Library of
Davidson College

TOWARDS AN EAST EUROPEAN MARXISM

MARC RAKOVSKI

Towards an East European Marxism

St. Martin's Press, New York

Copyright © Marc Rakovski 1978
Translation copyright © Allison & Busby 1978
All rights reserved. For information, write:
St. Martin's Press, Inc., 175 Fifth Ave., New York, N.Y. 10010
Printed in Great Britain
Library of Congress Catalog Card Number 77-18171
ISBN 0-312-81048-2
First published in the United States of America in 1978

Library of Congress Cataloging in Publication Data
Rakovski, Marc.
   Towards an East European Marxism.

   1. Russia – Economic conditions – 1976-   2. Europe, Eastern – Economic conditions. 3. Russia – Social conditions – 1970-   4. Europe, Eastern – Social conditions. I. Title.
HC336.25.R34   330.9'47'085   77-19171
ISBN 0-312-81048-2

Contents

1	Towards an East European Marxism	7
2	"Market Socialism" in Retrospect	18
	Who has an interest in economic reform?	20
	The ideology of the reformers	24
	The failure of the reformers	29
	The stabilisation of post-stalinist society	34
3	The Intellectuals	39
	Which intelligentsia?	43
	A feature of post-stalinist society	48
	The "sub-intelligentsia"	58
	Samizdat	62
	The various trends	69
4	The Two Systems in Action	73
	Economic organisation	77
	The class structure	83
	The consequences	86
	Technological development	91
	The structure of consumption	93
	Economic cycles	95
	Class struggle	98
5	The Detours of East European Marxism	105
	Marxism of the apparatus	106
	Leninism	110
	Trotsky, Bukharin and Stalin	115
	The Bolshevik canonisation of marxism	123
	The rebirth of marxism	130
	Underground marxism versus official marxism	134
	Index	139

1 Towards an East European Marxism

In spite of the disquieting proliferation of marxisms which are incapable of communicating with each other, there is still enough consensus on *the* key question — that of the attitude towards capitalist society — for us to be able to speak about "marxism" rather than "marxisms". Every marxist will admit that capitalism is a society which is based on class domination; that it must be eliminated; that its historical overcoming is not just an abstract imperative but the objective interest of one of the basic classes that goes to make up its social structure — the proletariat; and that the ultimate task of marxist theory is to lend its intellectual capabilities to the process of practical training by which the working class gains consciousness of its objective interests.

But where the other great world system, that of the East European countries and the USSR, is concerned, the various currents in marxism are incapable of even this minimal consensus. There are marxists who state that capitalist exploitation has been abolished in the Soviet-type societies; other marxists assume, on the contrary, that this type of society is based on the same mechanisms of exploitation as capitalism. There are others who accept the thesis that the East European working class has been freed from capitalist exploitation, but that political power has been expropriated by an all-powerful bureaucracy. Some marxists expect that the rapid development of the productive forces will create the economic basis of what they like to call "socialist democracy"; others believe that the Soviet type of development is a mere imitation of the economic and technological structure of capitalist accumulation, and consequently it cannot sustain any social relations other than those of capitalism. Some of them believe that the nationalisation of the means of production has opened the way towards an egalitarianism of a higher order; others believe that the inevitably hierarchical nature of the technical division of labour reproduces the same forms of inequality as those which prevail in capitalism. For some marxists, the Soviet type of economy is a non-market one; for others, it is a market economy. One marxist will insist on the social advantages that have been gained with the abolition of the market, while his opponent – also a marxist – asserts that no developed socialist economy can function without a market. And the most important thing is that the practical conclusions drawn from these arguments are likewise totally contradictory. Many marxists are inclined to accept the Soviet-type societies as they are; but there are also many who wish to see radical reforms or a social revolution. Some expect to see changes made from above, by the political leadership; others expect to see them come from below, from the working class; yet others place their hopes in the economic and technical experts.

But what is even more disquieting is the fact that, while in the West these tendencies which express different opinions on the main questions are in fact proliferating, at the same time in the East marxist thinking seems to be in the course of disappearing. The debate about the Soviet type of society is increasingly an internal affair of Western marxists. While it was always difficult for them to make intellectual contact with East European marxists, it is marxists themselves who are now difficult to find in Eastern Europe. A host of teachers of dialectical and historical materialism in the universities, a few nonconformist marxists in the underground, and there you have it. The mass of marxist intellectuals who in the forties and fifties did bridge the gap between the two has disappeared without trace.

Naturally, one has to seek the explanation in the structure of the historical development of Soviet-type societies. However, the reconstruction of the historical structure does not amount yet to a full explanation. The adverse social conditions, in fact, do explain why so many marxists have abandoned their convictions, but they do not explain why even the few who are determined to swim against the current feel acutely perplexed. Nevertheless, it is a fact that they feel perplexed; in the new situation they cannot make out what to do with the concepts which are given to them in the marxist tradition for the description and evaluation of Soviet-type societies.

The difficulties of the East European marxists can be better understood if we introduce some conceptual order into the multiplicity of marxist interpretations of Soviet-type societies. All these theoretical interpretations, including the most sophisticated of them, lead back to one of the three following basic types: that Soviet-type society is either socialism, or a transitional society made up of both capitalist and socialist elements, or it is capitalism.

According to the first of these conceptions, the social structure of the East European countries is determined by the abolition of private ownership of the means of production. The two most important consequences of this are the eradication of the exploiting classes and the fact that it becomes possible to plan and organise production at the level of the society as a whole. The first of these means a more equal distribution of income, a greater vertical mobility and real cultural democracy; the second means a more efficient allocation of resources, a more rational determination of social priorities, and a better satisfaction of collective needs. It is quite natural that this image of Soviet-type society should have become the official ideology of the East European states and the Western communist parties. But it goes further than that. Being fairly unspecific, it can easily be filled out with additions in order to gain the acceptance of critical fellow-travelling intellectuals. For example, they can add to this picture Soviet Russia's initial underdevelopment and the historical necessity for enforced industrialisation, thereby deducing that stalinism was the price which had to be paid for the creation of the economic basis of socialism. Or more probably they can supplement it with a description of the "distortions" at the highest political level and the violation of "leninist norms", and it turns into a criticism of the "personality cult". Furthermore, one need only add to it an account of the difficulties of the destalinisation process to make it compatible even with a categorical condemnation of "tragic errors" such as the occupations of Hungary and Czechoslovakia, the Gdansk massacre or the repression of nonconformist intellectual movements in the Soviet Union.

According to the second conception too, nationalisation of the means of production plays a central role. This constitutes the socialist element in Soviet-type development. However, the state does not only represent the general interest of the development of the productive forces, but also the particular interests of the bureaucrats: i.e. their privileges in income, life-style and prestige. In order to be able to defend these privileges from the other social groups (and above all from the working class), the bureaucracy tries to keep all its powers out of reach of public control. However, the corporate monopoly of the rights of disposition over the means of production is not sufficient to achieve this goal. In order for the privileges of state personnel to become inalienable and inheritable state property must be retransformed into private capitalist property. Hence the dual nature of the Soviet-type state: to the extent that it ensures development of the productive forces on the basis of state property, it is leading society towards socialism; to the extent that it gradually alienates itself from working class and offers growing opportunities for its bureaucrats to monopolise the exercise of proprietary rights, it is preparing for the restoration of capitalism. Such a contradiction cannot exist indefinitely: either socialism or capitalism will win. The bureaucracy's political domination will be replaced either by the self-management of the associated producers or by the class domination of the capitalist entrepreneurs.

This model of the transitional society was drawn by Trotsky during the thirties. Some of its constituent parts have had a great and lasting effect; for example, many themes from his critique of the bureaucracy reappeared in the thinking of the communist intelligentsia during the destalinisation period. But the whole conception has only ever been accepted by orthodox trotskyists. On the other hand, there is a large number of theories which are analogously structured. For example, during the heyday of economic reform in the East European countries some Western marxists tended to see the changes which were taking place as a manifestation of the contradictions between a socialist planning economy and a capitalist market economy.

The existence of certain institutional differences between the two systems is not denied entirely by the third conception. After all, Western Europe and Eastern Europe have arrived at contemporary capitalism by different historical routes: why be surprised, then, if the differences of the formation period have left their mark on the forms which have been reached? Nevertheless, the structural differences are not sufficiently great to enable us to determine two *sui generis* social formations. In all important aspects the two systems behave in the same way. In both, it is the reified logic of accumulation which determines the fate of all other social aims; in both, the consumer model and the technostructure are the same; the same hierarchical principles dominate the division of labour; and effective economic power is in the process of passing into the hands of a kind of technocracy, etc. This conception is the product of the end of the sixties; its origins are in the Western new left which has dissociated itself from the traditional left.

It is a well-known fact that for decades East European marxists thought about their society and their tasks in it in terms of the first conception. They took it for granted that the verbal marxism of official ideology was not a historical contingency but a "superstructual" reflection of the basic structure of the system. During the stalinist period they were not able even to think about distinguishing themselves from the institutionalised ideology. Autonomous non-official marxist thought only sprang up in the East European countries during the destalinisation period. And even then, there was no question of creating a marxism detached from the social base of official marxism. The aim was rather to purge marxism of its "dogmatic" residue and thus to reconstruct "authentic" marxism, the adequate ideology of *this* social system. Of course, the critique of theoretical "dogmatism" went hand in hand with the denunciation of political and sometimes institutional "distortions". But the unofficial marxists of this period never used the argument that in Soviet-type societies it is only the vocabulary of the official ideology that is socialist. Quite the opposite: the presupposition behind their criticism was that this is a fundamentally socialist society and that is why it is irreconcilable with phenomena like political authoritarianism, the ultra-dogmatic neglect of the needs of the masses or the substitution of controlled propaganda for culture.

At the time of the power struggles of the destalinisation period there was also an advantage stemming from the fact that the official and the unofficial marxism of the period argued from the same theoretical premises. This was precisely what enabled the latter to maintain some kind of influence over the outcome of struggles that were taking place among the various groups of the ruling class, though not the kind of influence which they hoped to have. But once the post-stalinist system had consolidated and the ruling class had established a new unity, this practical advantage quickly disappeared. There is no group of the ruling class that actually needs a public critique of official ideology any more. Marxists who seriously think that the Soviet-type societies are socialist ones and who are constantly calling on the leaders to realise socialist ideals are clearly a nuisance. The authorities respond to criticism with the argument of repression, and the marxists who previously sought to be the régime's genuine ideologues either bow to this repression or very quickly find themselves underground.

This is the explanation of the crisis in East European marxism. And it is very clear that it is a crisis that can be overcome only if a radical theoretical reorientation can be accomplished. As long as we start from the hypothesis that the Soviet-type societies are socialist, the only thing we can do is wait for the ruling class (or part of it) to call on our services again.

However, the other two traditional marxist conceptions likewise fail to offer any solution to the problem. The theory of the "transitional society" constantly swings between misplaced criticism and superficial excuses. On the one hand it forecasts that the state bureaucrats will turn into capitalist shareholders – but because this prophecy does not seem to be fulfilled it ends up with the opinion that although the bureaucracy has expropriated the proletariat at the political level, it still represents the dictatorship of the proletariat at the level of the means of production and economic accumulation. This apologetic undercurrent is all the more marked in trotskyism, since it contains no alternative to the Soviet type of property relations, technological development, division of labour and consumption. This oscillation between criticism and apologetics may well have been useful for these Western marxists who, fighting against fascism and in the strictly dichotomous world of the cold war, sought to avoid the trap of being identified either with stalinism or with anti-communism. But for East European marxists in the post-Stalin period who are trying to establish positions of intellectual autonomy, it simply makes the job more difficult.

And other versions of the "transitional society" idea are of no more use. It is the basic structure of the hypothesis which is wrong, not only its specific details. One cannot steer a non-contradictory course among the class relations of Soviet-type society by treating it as transitional. A society is transitional when its institutions are grouped round antagonistic power-centres and when the relationships between them are not regulated by legitimate and universally recognised mechanisms but by a more or less open struggle. In order to classify Soviet-type society as transitional, it is not enough to note that central planning exists simultaneously alongside another institution which in some ways resembles the capitalist market. One must also demonstrate that the first of these embodies, let's say, the economic power of the producers, while the second embodies the economic power of the managers and that regulated co-operation between the two is impossible in the long term. In this sense, Soviet Russia was genuinely a transitional society during the 1920s. The state apparatus had subjected urban Russia to its direct authority, without succeeding in doing the same for the countryside. The villages were in the hands of the peasant communities of private smallholders and did not recognise the local organisations of Soviet power. And the long-lasting coexistence of these two institutional systems was highly unlikely, because of the disastrous imbalance between industry and agriculture. But as soon as the state apparatus extended its power to the countryside by collectivising agriculture and created the economic base for this power by means of forced industrialisation, the class relations and the division of labour of Soviet Russia were integrated in a unified institutional system capable of reproducing itself. The same applies to the other East European countries after they turned into what are known as the "people's democracies".

The third conception certainly avoids the antinomies of the "transitional society" theory. And generally there are a lot of signs which obviously suggest a parallelism between Soviet-type and capitalist societies. Over the past two decades the similarities between the two systems have become more marked: the structure of consumer behaviour and the environment of everyday life in each society resemble each other more clearly, there is an obvious lack of essential differences in the technostructure and the hierarchical structures in the division of labour of the Soviet-type societies do not decompose. These similarities are very impressive, even if one can detect significant differences between the structure of consumer behaviour, the technostructure and hierarchical division of labour in the two types of societies. And their persuasive power is not weakened even by the fact that in certain other fields – for example in the case of the dynamic cycles and the characteristics of the employment situation – the differences are much more obvious than the similarities. But the closer the two systems resemble each other at the level of the everyday life of the working class, the more difficult it is to avoid asking the question, why has the working class succeeded in having an organised influence on its conditions of life in only one of the two systems? Why is it only Western capitalism that has a workers' movement, whether reformist or revolutionary? There can be no doubt that this is the key question for every marxism, and that also includes East European marxism, once it has managed to detach itself from the ruling class. A theory which makes no conceptual distinction between the two social systems, far from providing any solution to this problem, simply pushes it aside.

If marxists were simply content to draw up an inventory of the modern symptoms of alienation, they could certainly make good use of a theory which overlooks the differences between capitalist and Soviet-type societies. But marxism aims at something more than a general critique of civilisation; there is absolutely no reason why East Europeans addicted to *Kulturpessimismus* should search in marxism for concepts which they can get directly from openly conservative and irrationalist ideologies. These abound in the East European underground, and are much more popular there than marxism. But if marxism is to preserve its identity as a critical theory of society which is centred on the problems of the socialist workers' movement, it cannot then push aside the differences of institutional organisation and class structure between the two systems.

The communist and trotskyist descriptions of Soviet-type society do not enable East European marxists to break with the presuppositions of the official ideology. The description provided by the new left also fails to help them confront the specific obstacles which impede the renewal of the lost connection between marxism and its natural class base. If marxism is possible at all in Eastern Europe, it has to stand on a completely new theoretical foundation. The hypothesis which we are going to take as the point of departure for our investigations is therefore the following. Soviet-type society is neither socialist nor capitalist, nor is it a mixture of the two systems. It is a class society *sui generis*, a different kind of class society existing alongside capitalism.

Once one poses the problem in this manner, however, it becomes obvious that the difficult thing is not simply to give a marxist interpretation of the existing social system. In order to approach the fourth hypothesis which we have just set out above, it is necessary to reconsider the whole traditional structure of historical materialism. In the generally accepted framework of historical materialism it is impossible to give a description of a modern, non-transitional society where there is no capitalist private property but where the means of production are not at the collective disposal of the producers; where there is no bourgeoisie or proletariat but the population is still divided into classes; where economic priorities are not normally determined by the market, but neither are they chosen by means of rational discussion among the associated producers, and so on.

Of course, as Marx knew very well, the traditional societies which he termed "pre-capitalist" had all been like that. In his view it was only capitalism that could rise to the formation of private property and a class structure in the modern sense, and to a market with all the subjective and objective factors of production. But the more Marx underlines the historicity of the socio-economic categories within the framework of the capitalism/pre-capitalism couplet, the more obvious it becomes that his historicism is confined to this general contrast. Marx knew of only one non-capitalist form of modern development, communism, which he identified with the post-capitalist stage of general development; he did not define communism as a new configuration of categories such as property, classes, market, etc., but as their total disappearance.

The key to this limitation in Marx's historical perspective lies in his view of capitalism. Marx knew of many independent paths of pre-capitalist development. He says, for example, that tribal society was replaced by an "Asiatic mode of production" in ancient India and China, by an "antique mode of production" in mediterranean Europe, and by a "Germanic mode of production" in Europe north of the Alps. But when Western capitalism arrived, this multilinear development (to use a modern term) began to converge dramatically in one single direction. The capitalist world market brings about the disintegration of all the pre-capitalist systems and replaces them with the capitalist economy. As far as Marx is concerned, the general superiority of capitalism on the evolutionary scale is by no means only a simple historical fact. Capitalism does not simply eliminate all the other class societies, it brings to a head the whole development of class society. The economy separates itself from the non-economic institutions of society, and a purely economic class structure thereby emerges from the multiplicity of kinship, feudalism, religious affiliation, the guilds, etc.; private property emerges from the diversity of individual and collective rights of ownership; the technical division of labour emerges from the various forms of division of labour between sexes, generations, castes, orders, etc.; the market, based on the self-regulating mechanism of supply and demand, emerges from a market based on the network of mutual personal services, and various kinds of legal obligation, etc. While the economy remains within the bounds of the non-economic relations of society, its categories cannot help assuming a multitude of historical forms. But once this separation takes place, these earlier forms cannot continue their development: there can be only one purely economic type of class and property, only one type of technical division of labour, only one type of self-regulating market. Hence any further development of society must imply their elimination.

In spite of the key role which historicism played in Marx's thought, he was unable to avoid the simplifications of the unilinear evolutionism which dominated the social sciences of his period. Albeit for quite different reasons, ultimately his results are quite similar to those of the evolutionist anthropology and historiography of the period. In the eyes of the marxists of the Second International, he was a unilinear evolutionist. This interpretation was later to dominate the official historical materialism of the Comintern. Nevertheless, in the 1920s there were Western marxists in the communist parties belonging to the Comintern who polemically contrasted Marx's historicism with the unilinear evolutionism of the Second International theoreticians: and the influence of their line is still living in contemporary marxism. But the critique of the dominant marxist tradition was always content to demonstrate the existence of historicist ideas in Marx and to contrast them with later vulgarisations, without going into the internal contradictions of Marx's very conception of history. In this way one can get a much more sophisticated view of Marx's position concerning the traditional societies, but one can never overcome marxism's deep affinity with unilinear evolutionism. Hence one cannot introduce into this historical materialism the hypothesis that the Soviet-type societies are *sui generis* class societies existing alongside capitalism. Within the traditional structure of historical materialism there is no place for a modern social system which has an evolutionary trajectory other than capitalism and which is not simply an earlier or later stage along the same route.

2 "Market Socialism" in Retrospect

If we examine the historical turning-points which have occurred in the economic system of Soviet-type societies, we have the impression that its transformation has taken several diverging paths. Some of the smaller countries seem to have developed towards a kind of market system, at least so long as this does not meet with opposition from the bigger countries which have apparently maintained the stalinist system of administrative planning. But if, instead of examining the moments of political crisis, we examine long-term processes, the changes in question appear in a completely different light. The reforms are not radical enough, nor conservatism powerful enough, to obscure the very marked general tendency which exists amid the differing paths and rates of development in the various countries. Occasional interventions have gradually been replaced everywhere by stable regulators, and detailed instructions by simpler indices; planning in physical terms has given way to planning in financial terms; and in the maintenance of economic equilibrium, political mobilisation has given way to regularised co-ordinating mechanisms, etc.

The same ambivalence marks the ideological expression of this transformation. At the crucial moments "market socialism" has become the state ideology in those countries where far-reaching reform was gaining ground, while the conservative countries have mobilised their entire propaganda machine to fight it; but in this sphere, too, the long-term parallelism is quite obvious. Although the main ideas of "market socialism" have not been integrated everywhere into a coherent and dominant ideology, they nevertheless succeeded in making an appearance in all the East European countries between 1953 and 1968 (the years between the beginning of the decomposition of the stalinist régimes and the definitive consolidation of the post-stalinist régimes). There were numerous supporters everywhere of the doctrine that the market is a socially neutral tool for the co-ordination of economic activities (which can be used in any kind of society); that it is more efficient to allocate resources through the market than by administrative methods; and that the central concentration of the right of disposition over the means of production goes hand in hand with political authoritarianism, while decentralisation promotes political democracy. By the end of the 1960s at the latest, the ideology of "market socialism" had undergone a total defeat everywhere. But the defeat of the ideology only moderated the amplitude of oscillations round a general tendency, and has in no way changed the tendency itself.

Yet in one aspect, the eclipse of "market socialism" is definitely a landmark. The heyday of this ideology was the last period when the development of Soviet-type societies meant more for the politically committed intellectuals than just the actual empirical history of this particular part of the world. In the ideology of "market socialism" the *de facto* and the desired economic transformations appeared to be approximations of a new model of socialist economy – a model which was superior in every respect to the centralised type of planned economy – and as an example to be followed by all socialist movements. But since the consolidation of the post-stalinist régime, it is inconceivable that ideologies based upon the Soviet-type societies can establish similar claims. It is no accident that while the ideology of "market socialism" was at its height, the East European economic reforms stimulated fierce polemics among Western marxists, but since the fall of this ideology, transformations in more or less the same direction taking place in the East European economic systems scarcely raise any interest among them.

From a purely theoretical point of view this de-ideologisation of development should be seen as positive, for in fact the debate about market socialism simply hindered understanding of those objective processes which in fact called this ideology to life. The issues at the centre of the debate ("Is socialism compatible with the market?" "Is it possible without the market?") had very little to do with the realities of the economic reform. They are, of course, vitally important issues for marxism's general social theory, and from this point of view it is by no means a good thing that they have since been simply forgotten. But it is clearly an advantage that the interpretation of the development of Soviet-type society is no longer impeded by the debate on these above-mentioned issues. So far, marxists have never succeeded in examining Soviet-type society in itself and for itself. The attempt to find out objectively about the East European experience has always been confused with the question of what the experience means to revolutions which have been won or lost or are still to come in other parts of the world. But for the first time, it now becomes natural to take Soviet-type society, in the same way as capitalist society, simply for what it is: a modern class society.

The normative aspects of "market socialism" are consciously set aside in this chapter: the ideology of "market socialism" is treated simply as the ideology of a particular social group. The questions we deal with are: who it was that constituted this group, why they sought to advance their interests through the re-establishment of market mechanisms and, finally, why they were defeated.

Who has an interest in economic reform?

The ideology of "market socialism" tried to claim that the reform which was associated with this ideology was dictated by a general economic rationale, and not by pressure from a particular social group. But not even the most extreme neo-liberal eulogies of the market ever succeeded in making us forget completely the fact that reform poses the question not only of the general performance capabilities inherent in various economic systems, but also the question of power. However modest they may be, reforms always involve a redistribution of decision-making rights among the various levels of economic management. Even if all the other changes affected all social groups in the same way, it would still be true that because of this shift some of them would have a greater interest in the changes than others, namely those whose power and prestige would increase as a result of the reforms. The political élite of the ruling class obviously is not among these groups, since all power was in its own hands under the previous system. We can also exclude all those groups which do not belong to the ruling class: no reform programme, however bold, has ever gone so far as to suggest that even a portion of economic power might be handed over to groups which previously were totally outside the orbit of the preparation and making of decisions. The idea that the working class should share in economic power has occurred to only those people who do not support reforms for their own sake but with a longer-term aim in view. The social forces behind the "market socialism" ideology must therefore be situated somewhere between these two poles: they would appear to come from that segment of the ruling class which extends from the decision-makers at enterprise level to those who, although they are decision-makers at the national economic level, nevertheless remain outside the political élite.

It is not a contingent element of the picture that the dividing lines are so vague. The part of the ruling class which has an interest in the reforms is heterogeneous, it is a composite of groups whose clear contours cannot be mapped out. Most of these groups can only be defined by their relative positions in the economic hierarchy. The only exception is the group whose members are generally termed "experts". No matter where they are placed in this hierarchy, the experts are linked with each other through their ability to solve technical problems, not merely through the manipulation of personal relations within hierarchically structured institutions. The primary criterion of their selection is naturally their professional competence, and ideological and political conformity is a secondary precondition. It is the experts who created that permanent refrain of the "market socialism" ideology, "scientific" competence as opposed to political criteria.

Experts reach the political élite only in exceptional cases, though this opportunity is open even to lower-level economic managers. The introduction of a market system offers them the promise of a clear growth in their power. In a market system of economic regulation, enterprises are subject to stricter demands on the promptness and sensitivity of their perception of the changes going on around them and on the precision of their adaptive reactions than they would be in a centrally administered economy. Hence the decline in the part played by political routine in economic decision-making, and the growth of the part played by professional expertise. It is hardly surprising that at every level of the hierarchy the staunchest supporters of the reforms are the experts.

The supporters of "market socialism" also include many lower-level economic decision-makers: the directors of production and service enterprises. The introduction of market mechanisms enables them to avoid being reduced to the position where they simply carry out tasks which are always changing and at the same time have already been determined in detail; they do not have to wait for the central economic management in every case to make available to them the necessary factors of production which are required at each moment for the current task, but can instead solve general economic tasks which, for the most part, are under their permanent control. They have a certain amount of capital at their disposal and have to make a certain amount of profit. It is they who decide how to exploit the available capital to obtain the desired result. This is of course only an ideal picture; it did not occur in the actual practice of the reform — not even in its ideology — except in a somewhat vague way. But this ideal picture helps us to understand the specific situation of the enterprise directors in relation to the sectoral and functional organs of the central management apparatus.

Guaranteeing the conditions for the profitable running of enterprises is a relatively irrelevant task for these organs. Their major responsibility is to supply the national economy with certain necessary commodities, to maintain a macro-equilibrium in money and goods, to contain the tendency for prices to rise, to guarantee full employment and the rapid growth of priority sectors, etc. The execution of these tasks in accordance with the interests of the central authorities is always a constraint upon the profit maximisation strategy of enterprises. A particular enterprise may benefit from a major streamlining of its product structure. But the minister in overall charge may as a result lose the strategic position he obtains from being able to satisfy all the demand in his sphere. Another enterprise may find it beneficial to close one of its factories and transfer its capital to another part of the country. But the local municipal government will then have to face new problems in the employment situation. Yet another enterprise may succeed in tripling productivity by doubling the average wage. But in this case, it will subject the labour authorities to perhaps irresistible pressure from other enterprises which are not in a position to raise wages, etc.

We can easily understand that if the whole process were to be determined by this contradiction alone, the lower-level economic managers would constantly be under general pressure from the whole hierarchical apparatus, and would be unable to obtain greater autonomy except to a very small degree. But the same contradiction is reproduced at the higher levels and branches of the management hierarchy. The introduction of the market not only decreases the enterprise directors' dependence on the central apparatus, it also promises to redistribute the remaining rights of supervision among the various rungs in the apparatus. In an ideal market model, for example, the power of the so-called "functional" departments (and chiefly the ministry of finance) would clearly increase at the expense of the sectoral departments. Some institutions would extend their sphere of competence, others would lose some of their rights of supervision over enterprise activities but would be compensated by a similar reduction in their dependence on higher-level institutions. There is a considerable variation, according to the country and to the various stages of reform, in the overall composition of the management organs which have a positive interest in the redistribution of the rights of supervision. Hence, at different times and places, different groupings of the middle and higher economic management will be actual supporters of reforms. Nevertheless, there are always supporters of the reform to be found somewhere in the central apparatus.

So far we have only looked at the interests involved in changes in the management system from the point of view of the exercise of power. Let us now look at the advantages which accrue in terms of individual consumption. Even under the old system, a rise in the hierarchy meant a significant rise in money income; but because of the chronic poverty of the consumer goods market and the absolute underdevelopment of services, this income was in itself incapable of generating the privileges suitable to that level of exercising power. Hence the separate system in the distribution of consumer goods for supplying the needs of the upper stratum of the ruling class. This system did not function according to the principles of commodity circulation but according to those of distribution in kind. And even products which could be bought for money were not sold like ordinary commodities. In order to make a purchase, it was not enough simply to have the necessary amount of money: entry into these shops was a controlled privilege. The expansion of the production of consumer goods creates a new situation for those strata of the rulers who previously have been excluded from these privileges. Economic autonomy grows and the system of material incentives that goes with it causes their money incomes to shoot up. The more abundant and varied supply of commodities enables them to catch up with the élite in terms of controlled privileges, consumption and life-style, In this sphere too it is the experts' interests which are the most evident. They are kept further away from the privileged distribution system, yet at the same time they are the most self-consciously aspiring to the life and consumer style of the Western middle classes.

The ideology of the reformers

When all this is considered, it is not difficult to understand why the economic reform programme sought its own justification, at least at its heyday, in the ideology of "market socialism". But if we think harder, we realise that we are confronted here precisely with the real difficulty. The reform programme was accompanied by an ideology which aimed at replacing bureaucratic linkages in the management of the economy with the self-regulation of the market; but the programme itself never aimed this far.

When one examines the practical reform projects which were supposed to put the market mechanisms into action, one comes across proposals such as the following: that the centrally determined duties of the enterprise should be limited to the size of the gap between receipts and expenditures; that similar enterprises should be placed under equal conditions of competition; that centrally fixed prices (including the price of labour power as well) should be limited to the politically necessary minimum; and that the income of economic decision-makers should be dependent on the efficiency of their activities in economic terms, provisions for greater differentials in wages should be made etc. All these proposals hinge on the question of which economic regulators the central authorities can use to direct the enterprise towards the realisation of the general goals of which these authorities are the representative agents. To the extent that the changes envisaged relegate the detailed and contingent forms of central regulation to the background, they in fact reduce the enterprise directors' dependence on the central management apparatus. But these are only changes in the dependency linkages within the regulatory system; they do not even touch upon the basic institutional underpinnings of that dependence. Not even the boldest programmes went so far as to call in question the institutional framework of the Soviet-type economy in which enterprise directors are appointed, dismissed, rewarded and punished by the central authorities – that is to say, by the institutions of the very same hierarchy that is responsible for supplying the national economy with commodities and for guaranteeing full employment etc., which has a state budget at its disposal, and which uses the banking system to manipulate financial credit and uses the party and the unions to manipulate the political consensus and the harmonising of interests.

But without the disassembly of this hierarchical system, there can be no successful transformation of the enterprises into profit-maximising market organisations, however decentralised the regulating mechanisms are. Whether or not the central authorities renounce their formal right to give *ad hoc* instructions to the enterprise directors, they invariably preserve their institutional power to use pressure in order to force him to deviate from the optimum economic strategy determined by forecasts based upon market criteria. The corollary to the central authorities' power to do this is their responsibility for compensating tame enterprises for the opportunities they miss:

if conflicts between the desire to maximise the benefits of the market and the priorities of the central apparatus take place regularly enough, such enterprises can systematically improve their situation without even attempting to respond to the demands of the market.

Why is there this discrepancy between ideology and the practical programme? We can dismiss immediately the most plausible-looking hypothesis, that the more radical implications of the reform were concealed for tactical considerations. If the reform's supporters were in fact so much on their guard against divulging the details of their programme, how then do we explain their careless frankness about the pronouncement of the ultimate aims of the reform? And what does it mean that the reform programme was cautious? It was timid if we compare it with the ideology of "market socialism", but it was certainly still too bold if we compare it with the limits of the ruling class's tolerance.

The real factors which kept the social forces behind the reform from really thinking over, in public, the institutional preconditions for the introduction of market-type self-regulatory mechanisms were quite different. These forces wanted the market, but they did not want to dismantle the institutional relations of dependence which prevent the market from dominating the co-ordination of economic activities. They wanted the market because they hoped to have equal power with the old political élite and to catch up with the latter's personal consumption. But they did not want the relations of dependence to disintegrate because, although these relations limit their freedom, they also shelter them.

We have already mentioned that the economic managers above enterprise level felt ambivalent about the introduction of the market, and this does not require further clarification. What is interesting is that we encounter the same kind of ambivalence among lower-level management. Enterprises which are directly dependent on the central management apparatus are less free to make spectacular business deals than the autonomous enterprises, but they are less answerable for the consequences of a bad deal. The state as boss is always there to lend distressed but tame clients a hand with tax exemptions, further credit, preferential prices, etc. Given a free hand by the state, some enterprises could, because of their location, technology, size, etc., make profits far above average; other enterprises, however, would have to reduce production, incur large deficits or meet difficulties of adaptation. In the current system, the central economic management apparatus maintains a balance among unequal situations in enterprises and sectors by blocking the expansion of the former and rescuing the latter from collapse, through the transfer of material resources from one to the other. It is therefore reasonable to expect (and this is in fact what happened where the reform actually took off) that directors of enterprises which are well prepared for market competition will exercise a great deal of pressure to have these ties of dependence loosened, while the directors of enterprises which are ill-adapted to competition will try to block this process.

The situation is complicated further by the presence of a non-economic component among the risks inherent in the economic activity of the enterprises. Enterprise directors who are freed from the tutelage of the central authorities face not only the possibility that they will run up a deficit, but also the possibility of a steep increase in the level of workers' resistance. In this respect, too, the central apparatus fulfils a dual function. It sets a limit to the exploitation of workers by enterprise directors, and it intervenes in order to guarantee security of employment and stable wages, even gradual wage rises. But the central apparatus also gives protection to enterprise directors who are faced with workers' demands beyond this minimum. It has the means to atomise the workers' efforts to advance their interests; and when in spite of everything there is a polarisation in an industrial conflict, it is capable of rapidly breaking the workers' organised resistance and of equally rapidly satisfying the most urgent of the demands.

If the hierarchy above enterprise level were to disintegrate and lose its authority (and it is a hierarchical order which in itself alone discharges the functions of regulating economic growth and equilibrium and is also responsible for the maintenance of political consensus and the harmonising of interests), the workers would have a chance to institute and consolidate their own counter-organisations, and to co-ordinate the running of them. Of course, it is not only the workers who would be able to organise themselves in this hypothetical state of affairs but all other social groups as well. But the various groups do not have an equal interest in the possibilities of organising themselves. Those groups which make up the ruling class have a share in power by virtue of their very functioning in the hierarchical system of the social division of labour. What they gain in opportunities to organise themselves is not enough to counterbalance what they lose as a result of the extended opportunities of these social groups which remain completely excluded from power if the power hierarchy is preserved. If the lower and middle-level economic managers and the experts around them organised themselves, they might perhaps improve their standing a little in comparison with the political élite, but they would lose a much greater amount of ground to the working class. Rather than go so far as to break the ties of dependence which chain them to the central management apparatus, they submit to it voluntarily in order to prevent the workers beneath them from breaking free. Their aim is not a society in which opposing social groups have the means to conduct an organised struggle against each other, in order to advance their particular interests in economic and political conflicts. What they want is to get a better position within the existing system, where everything is gained by means of the amorphous pressure which the conflicting groups can bring to bear on the central apparatus.

The fact that the reform programmes petered out before the institutionalised relations of dependency shows that far from being the nucleus of a new ruling class, the social forces behind the reform were simply a subordinate part of the old one. They tried to better their own position within the old kind of class domination, but not represent a new kind. This conclusion accords perfectly with the long-term trend in the economic transformation of the East European societies. But how can the short-term deviations from this trend be explained? The problem is now reversed. In this case, what needs to be explained is not the moderation of the practical programmes but the radicalism of the ideology. Why did the supporters of the reform demand the market so vehemently if they were not prepared to demand the institutional conditions that would enable it to be introduced?

The failure of the reformers

The historical period during which the "market socialism" ideology grew, blossomed and withered was the roughly fifteen-year period of transition from the stalinist to the post-stalinist régime.

In the economic sphere, stalinism meant accumulation at any price, the concentration of virtually the whole of the social surplus product for these tasks, and the whole life of society was subordinated to these aims. The realisation of these accumulation tasks created a permanent disequilibrium and oppression in whole areas of social life such as consumption, free time and private life. The combined means of ideological and physical terror were employed for the purposes of this total mobilisation. A symbolic ideological relationship was created between everyday actions, however trivial, and the basic principles of socialism: the ideology portrayed any non-conformist actions as resistance and sabotage, which invited terror in reply. This enabled the political élite to exercise unlimited power over all social groups and strata.

In spite of its chronic disequilibrium, the stalinist policy of accumulation succeeded in creating large-scale modern industry. But it was this very success that made the economy increasingly vulnerable to these disequilibria. Although terror was good at sucking the social surplus product out of agriculture in order to turn it over to industry, or at containing individual consumption, it was quite impossible to tackle the internal imbalances of an industrial structure which had become highly complex, by exorcising ideological deviations or by chasing after the alleged class enemy. Another factor acting against the continuation of the stalinist system was the fact that the ruling class was obliged to come to terms gradually with the inability of any of its subaltern groups to feel safe from the self-generating mechanisms of terror.

Of course, these mechanisms are difficult to interrupt. But

once it stopped, the whole previous organisation of the economy became a problem. One could no longer resort to the terrorist mobilisation of the whole economy in order to eliminate the most dangerous imbalances at the price of creating others. Once the terrorist pressure on private life is eased, the demand for a rise in real incomes cannot be turned down. There is effective demand for consumer goods, and this necessitates more subtle ways to balance the economy. Hence the need for the economy to be more adaptable, to develop a differentiation in the economic decision-making levels and to obtain a freer circulation of commodities, cash and information among the lower-level units. The interruption of mass terror automatically entails a reform of the economic system.

In fact the reform progressed extremely timidly during its first years. It was confined for a time to a prudent simplification of the management structure and a not too radical reduction in the number of indices. It took a long and bitter debate before even the "law of value" could be admitted to exist to a certain extent in the Soviet-type economy. And it needed even more time to get the idea of "giving greater scope" to the law of value accepted. At the outset, therefore, the first reforms were not commensurate to the desirable size and speed of the changes already necessary. This is why the first years of the destalinisation period were dominated not so much by a reform of the system of economic regulation as by the conversion of the old machinery towards new ends: there were repeated attempts to use decrees in order to achieve a dramatic reallocation of social resources from heavy to light industry, from producer goods to consumer goods.

At this time the new power constellation that might spring from the redistribution of economic decision-making rights was not yet a motive in the struggle within the ruling class. The question of power only sprang up in the context that once mass terror was eliminated, the most discredited part of the responsible political élite had to leave. But this in itself was enough to cause a deep shock; in two countries, Poland and Hungary, this process resulted in a temporary power vacuum, giving grounds for the expression of popular anger caused by poverty and oppression.

If we leave aside the remnants of the classes that sought the restoration of capitalism, the dramatic events of 1956 had only two protagonists: the political élite, which was disintegrating into antagonistic factions, and "the people". The strata of the ruling class below the political élite were absorbed by "the people"; the idea of economic reform had not matured enough yet to enable them to offer society a global alternative according with their own particular interests.

The development of the crisis was interrupted by military force, and this pre-empted any thoughts of reform. But not forever. The system of mass terror was not re-established, so the old methods of overcoming economic disequilibrium by means of political mobilisation were not viable any more. Consumer needs could not remain systematically neglected. However, the administrative improvement of production structures was not sufficient in itself to guarantee a continued supply of commodities to the economy nor a rise in the level of consumption. From time to time either the producer or the consumer industries were blocked by a lack of supplies, which forced the central authorities to allocate all the available resources to either one or the other. The economic and social tensions increasingly pointed to the need for reform. And in fact, after a temporary hesitation, the reform movement from then on progressed unimpeded until the end of the 1960s. It was during this period that the shift of power positions began, in which the lower- and middle-level economic managers and the "experts" around them became a power factor within the ruling class.

In the countries where in 1956 the most severely compromised representatives of stalinism were toppled from power, the change took place in a relatively continuous manner. The élite of the ruling class learned to separate the defence of its privileges from any attempt to restore stalinism, while the rising strata learned to conceal the political implications of their economic programmes. This mutual prudence strongly reduced the likelihood of sudden crises. But the tendency towards the decentralisation of economic management turned out to be irresistible also in those countries where the renovation of the political élite did not take place, since the reforming forces had the support of the majority of the population everywhere. The change promised a more abundant and diverse supply of consumer goods, a reduction of political constraints in the sphere of employment, and an improvement in the quality of leisure services. All this clearly meant a rise in the standard of living for the whole population. Any attempt by the leadership to hold back the reforms appeared to the masses as an attempt to restore stalinism. However, the general popularity of their programme deluded the rising groups of the ruling class into thinking that they had been called upon to run society as a whole, and to replace the political élite grouped around the summit of the party apparatus. This is the illusion which the "market socialism" ideology expressed.

Nothing demonstrates the fact that it was only an illusion better than the lack of a practical programme that could match, in terms of institutional change, the desire to install a market economy. But though the idea of "market socialism" remained utopian, as an ideology it was nevertheless capable at certain moments of becoming a serious practical force and of having a real effect on social behaviour and attitudes. There was a particularly strong temptation for the rising groups of the ruling class to think of themselves as the legitimate heirs of the political élite in those countries where the élite still represented the old stalinist past. It was no accident that "market socialism" found its most aggressive expression in Czechoslovakia. The Czechoslovakian crisis of 1968 was different from the Hungarian and Polish crises of 1956, to the extent that the attempt to change the political élite went hand in hand with an attempt to change the system of economic management; and the two processes helped each other.

The occupation of Czechoslovakia interrupted the growth of the reform movements and announced to the whole of Eastern Europe that the "market socialism" ideology was finished. But military intervention was not the only cause of its defeat. At least as important a factor was the erosion of the mass support which the reformers of the early 1960s had been able to count on. Paradoxically, military intervention in the political process made it clear to the people of the East European countries that they were no longer threatened with a return to stalinism.

During this extraordinarily brutal intervention no attempt was made to revive the mobilisation of everyday life or to reduce the consumer level to a minimum. So the breaking up of the reform movement even won a certain kind of popularity, chiefly with the working class. Once the working class's consumer needs were recognised, its attitude no longer reflected a correlation between economic reform and a general rise in the standard of living. In the eyes of the working class, decentralisation of the management system was now associated with the differentials in that rising standard. And there is no doubt that the main beneficiaries of the changes were the economic and technical experts and the lower- and middle-level managers.

It is not that the difference between the standard of living of the ruling class as a whole and that of the working class has increased absolutely over the last two decades. In this comparison the attempt to weigh the absolute differences would be misleading anyway. If the case is that the living standards of the previously handicapped strata were roughly at subsistance level and that later their living standards rose significantly, then the purely quantitative comparison with the position of the privileged classes becomes meaningless. Furthermore, in the stalinist period the difference between the living standards of the élite of the ruling class and those of the working class was bigger even in purely quantitative terms than between that of the working class and the lower- and middle-level managers after the reforms. But the higher living standards of the strata which were behind the reforms is much more visible, even to the general public. The social group in question is much bigger than the old élite. This is precisely the group which directly exercises power over the working class and thus at least a part of its membership is in constant contact with the workers. The living standards of this group are reached by consuming from the same general market as the working class, i.e. they buy goods which are in principle also accessible to the workers. However, the workers do not have sufficient money to buy them. And what is more, the consumption of these goods takes place not in the closed world of the old élite, but at least partly in front of the general public, in a kind of ostentatious consumption.

The élite of the ruling class has turned these shifts to its own advantage and has counterattacked openly. It presents itself as the protector of the working class against those strata which are trying to enrich themselves at the latter's expense. The groups under attack have put up no serious resistance, not even in the countries where the reforms went a relatively long way. In fact they too understand that they are not representatives of the working class against the political élite but that, on the contrary, it is they who need the élite to protect them from expressions of worker discontent. They have therefore accepted the supremacy of the political élite. They have given up their radical ideology; all they want now is to improve their position as a subordinate group of the ruling class.

The stabilisation of post-stalinist society

It was not only the counterattack by the political élite that put an end to the second stage of the reforms. The effect of the strife between the working class and the lower- and middle-level economic managers was to re-establish the real unity of the ruling class, which had been shaken in the years of the transitional reform period. The ruling-class strata below the political élite have gradually realised that they too have a great interest in preserving the hierarchy of the central apparatus. The top leadership does not allow them to reduce the level of the workers' wages and employment below a certain critical limit. But it does guarantee them a slow rise in their own salaries and ensure their own stability of employment. And at the same time as justifying its own very existence by claiming that it is acting in the interests of the working class, the central apparatus prevents the workers from carrying out any organised resistance to the pressure brought to bear on them by these lower- and middle-level managers. If the enterprise directors had been invested with autonomous economic power, then in principle there could be organised economic struggle against the power apparatus. But if on the contrary their power is a subordinate part of the power of the united politico-economic apparatus, which alone governs economic growth, the political consensus and the harmonising of particular interests, then any opposition to them assumes a political character and invites intervention from the repressive machinery of the state.

Another important factor in the re-establishment of ruling-class unity has been homogenisation of its life-style. The attractions of the style which is linked with the system of controlled privileges has diminished, even for the political élite. Meat has appeared in shops open to the general public; even the state-supplied limousine-with-chauffeur has disadvantages compared with the private car. The élite, whose cash incomes have been growing too, have begun to turn towards those "Western" type goods and services which are available on the market. The system of controlled privileges has begun to vanish slowly. No group forming part of the élite would find it easy to redevelop such a system again by trying, within the framework of an attempt to restore stalinism, to reverse radically the new trends of consumer behaviour. The formal privileges were an organic part of the general state of poverty during the post-revolutionary and post-war years, which had to be accepted by the whole population as a given condition. The original point of the system was to enable the élite to draw, from the threadbare stock of consumer goods, the minimum without which they would be unable to carry out their management functions. Later on this system was to adapt itself to the rising demands of the élite, but of course could not keep pace with the differentiation and dynamism of the rising market.

If the lower- and middle-level managers are not interested in breaking with the élite, then the élite is not interested in restoring stalinism. But the most important aspect of the post-stalinist consolidation must be sought elsewhere. There has been an irreversible change not only in the structure of working-class consumption but also in its economic function. Under stalinist economic management, workers' consumption was simply an administrative supply problem: part of the annual social product had to be subtracted from the amount used for accumulation. The smaller this part was, the quicker the economy grew. In the post-stalinist state, on the other hand, a balanced rise in the consumer standards of the working class is an integral precondition of balanced economic growth. If the rise in demand for consumer goods remains behind the envisaged figure, then large economic sectors become unable to continue producing at a desirable level. The result is a slow-down in the rate of economic growth and increasing difficulties in the sphere of employment. To attack the level of mass consumption so far achieved would thus involve the risk not only of provoking the people's discontent, but also of disrupting the economic system.

However, once rising mass consumption is integrated in the normal operation of the economy, the decentralisation of decision-making becomes partly irreversible. Once they had departed from the system of central decisions in physical indices and from administrative supply quotas, there were no returns to this system in any country. A country like Rumania, where even today the drive for the most rapid accumulation is enforced against all the rational norms of micro-economics, is an exception. The typical cases are Poland and the German Democratic Republic, where a relatively circumspect simplification of the system of directives has been combined with the establishment of giant trusts which are relatively easy to control.

In none of the East European countries and at no stage of the reform were the indicators of success established by the central authorities reduced to profit alone. In recent years they have become even more complex in the majority of the countries involved. But the retreat has not gone so far that the detailed production plan in physical indices has been restored. And we must expect that the pressure exercised on the economic management system by the development of mass consumption will be powerful enough in the long term to give rise to a new drive for decentralisation. Demand becomes diversified and more variable, shortening the socially acceptable time-limit for adapting production to demands. In order to satisfy this demand, decision-making rights must increasingly be allocated to the managers of producer and service enterprises, so that they can follow changes in demand more freely and rapidly. This decentralisation of the regulating system will progress more easily as it becomes clear to everyone that lower- and middle-level economic managers will not try to exploit their strengthened position by making a frontal attack on the existing institutional system of dependence.

It is unlikely that future crises in Soviet-type society will spring from the ruling class. There is nothing in our view of the consolidated post-stalinist society which would lead us to expect that any eventual changes in the relative positions of the various ruling-class groups will raise the question of power again. If there is a new division in the ruling class at all, it will be the consequence of the crisis rather than its cause.

But are there not changes in the position of the *ruled* class in the post-stalinist system which cannot be accommodated at all, and is the adaptation to this system only possible through serious crises? We are still at the beginnings of this development. The changes which are taking place have not yet revealed their scope, nor their chances of converging and amplifying each other. But all the changes are enormous and in some cases the political consequences are already visible. Politically the least ambiguous phenomenon is the appearance and continuous reproduction of intellectual nonconformism. The changes taking place in the situation of the working class are evident too, but they are more difficult to interpret.

The workers did not get what they were promised from "market socialism" any more than the lower-level economic managers did. But even they have not gone unrewarded in post-stalinist development. Slowly but clearly, their standard of living continues to rise. In East European workers' households the accessories of the consumer society so well-known in the West are beginning to appear (including the family car), although in most cases their technical standard is lower than that of their Western original, the presentation poorer, and the servicing of them less abundant. No doubt this process will produce the negative symptoms of the consumer society here, too: life reduced to the pursuit of objects, overtime, moonlighting.

Once this is said, however, it would be a serious mistake to look at post-stalinist society as a poor but basically faithful reproduction of capitalist consumer society. For the working class in capitalist countries, the alternatives are as follows: expansion of individual consumption beyond any reasonable limits, or collective control of the conditions of life and labour. And they are real alternatives, not simply a confrontation between ideals and reality. The Western working class is organised, even if it is obviously still true that it cannot transform its counter-institutions into the basis of social organisation as a whole without overthrowing the capitalist system. But in Soviet-type society, social activity is co-ordinated and controlled by an institutional system which makes any kind of self-organisation impossible, and in which workers' resistance is confined to the level of individual behaviour. In this context, the accumulation of personally owned objects is not an alternative, but a means towards the only conceivable form of autonomy — individual autonomy. The worker who has some economic assets is in a better position to stand up to his superiors and to put up with the temporary economic losses which go with a change of job, whether voluntary or enforced. These advantages are especially clearly demonstrated in the younger generation of workers who are just entering production. Young workers with a strong family background have a greater freedom of movement among various jobs and skills, and even between work and temporary idleness — for the family budget has become more flexible, and the young worker's wage is no longer absolutely essential to the maintenance of the household.

What are the consequences of this change? We can by no means be sure of seeing anything like the revolt of young production-line workers at Fiat, Renault and General Motors. But what is certain is that the rise in the material and cultural standards of the East European working class will produce a new situation. It will intensify the pressures on the institutional system of Soviet-type society and will present it with new problems of adaptation, problems to which there are as yet no tried and tested solutions.

3 The Intellectuals

For the Western left, the choice of being for or against the Soviet experiment used to have not only a political dimension but a moral one too, and sometimes even an existential one. If one was for it, then it was more than to pass a historical judgment, one also accepted the responsibility for its crimes – but of course one accepted a similar kind of responsibility if one was against. The tragic thing about this situation was that it had something inevitable about it: one could not decline the choice. It seemed, or it really was the case, that anyone who tried to avoid the choice by appealing to considerations of a higher order was, in doing so, making the choice in any case, but without the courage to face its consequences.

It was a truly dichotomous world; the problem of consciousness was irredeemably unilateral. What happened in the Soviet Union forced the question of moral responsibility on left-wing intellectuals, but the responsibility they had to take was not for the fate of individuals who were caught in the historical events. For the Western left, the moral problem of the terror trials was not whether to leave the accused anarchists, Mensheviks and Communists to their fate. The people who tried to do something for the accused were by no means confronted with the moral problem at this abstract level, or else they had already solved it at some other level quite apart from the problem of personal solidarity. They were either simply Western anarchists, trotskyists and social democrats trying to save the lives of individuals who were their opposite numbers in the Soviet Union, or they were well-known intellectuals who because of their clearly pro-Soviet behaviour were in a good position to try and help this or that writer or scientist.

The situation today is in reverse. Although the decision to choose socialism and reject the Soviet experience is not always easy from the point of view of political practice, it is no longer a moral dilemma. On the other hand, solidarity with the victims of repression has confronted the contemporary Western left with serious problems of conscience. Anyone who opposes the USSR in the name of socialism cannot simply confine himself to the defence of particular persons or groups. He does not want to perpetuate the coexistence of the two systems, nor has he any scruples that need smoothing over because of co-operation with the Soviet state. What he wants is to supersede historically Soviet-type society as such. He therefore cannot avoid moral responsibilities, he has a duty to lend his solidarity to anyone risking his freedom or sometimes his life in the struggle to achieve this historic aim.

However, there is not one tendency on the Western left which is in a position to name any tendency in the Russian cultural and political underground with which it could identify itself unreservedly. The anti-Western, anti-cultural phraseology of Russian national messianism is much too reminiscent of antediluvian European conservatism for these intellectuals to be attracted, even when they do have some sympathy for romantic *Kulturkritik*. That part of the opposition which appeals to marxism in a purified form, to "leninist norms", is simply waiting for social changes to come from above, and this makes them unacceptable to Western marxists. Those who call for the ethical rebirth of man combine idealist mysticism with a contempt for the unregenerated *Massenmensch* and therefore put themselves in opposition to the democratic traditions of the European left. And finally, those who indulge in naïve eulogies of the benefits of Western liberalism are going against the beliefs of all left-wing intellectuals, whatever their ideology.

The most natural solution to this dilemma for the Western left seems to be to support the heroic gesture as such, but at the same time to make a critique of its political content. This is an obvious solution, because however unacceptable they may find the ideology attached to a particular gesture, the gesture itself of course commands the genuine admiration of the Western left. The reason is that in the West, it is extremely difficult to realise the unity of life and radical thought. There, radical ideas are themselves turned into commodities: far from involving any risk, producing them can be a very profitable business. But the radical intelligentsia of Eastern Europe, if indeed it is truly radical, does not encounter this kind of danger.

There is a kind of cult of the "dissident intellectual" in the process of formation in the West, which can be compared with the cult of the terrorist *Narodniks* at the end of the nineteenth century. But the intellectuals of that period, in their search for a model unity between thought and personal destiny, found it much easier to interpret the example set by the assassins of tsars, grand dukes and ministers of police. The terrorists acted, rather than reflecting on the meaning of their actions; and Russia was far enough away from Western Europe at that time for Western intellectuals to consider simply the abstract model of behaviour which these actions seemed to represent. However, with the dissident Soviet intelligentsia, action is nothing but reflection itself; it is by thinking aloud, by demanding and creating a public audience for their ideas that nonconformist intellectuals act in the USSR. That is why a list of excuses, made in a defensive tone of voice, creeps into the West's hero-worship: Soviet intellectuals are starved of information particularly on the realities of the Western world, they react to the lies of official propaganda in a way which is quite understandable but of which we do not approve, etc., etc.

This vicious circle of idolisation and paternalistic understanding can only be broken by means of an examination of Soviet intellectual nonconformism in its specific social context. But the conceptual schemes which the Western left intelligentsia normally calls upon in order to interpret what happens in the East European countries fail to come to grips with this whole phenomenon. Those who think of Soviet-type society as some kind of socialism can perhaps explain the rise of internal communist oppositions. Those who see it as a transitional society, as a mixture of capitalist and socialist properties, can account for the rise of restorationist movements. But the intellectual nonconformism of the 1970s is neither one thing nor the other. In contrast with the opposition communism of the decade after Stalin's death, the nonconformist intellectuals no longer denounce the "deformations" of the system but the system itself. And yet the nonconformist intellectuals – even those among them who in their absolutely hopeless situation take refuge in reactionary utopias – are not representatives of the former ruling class. There is no explanation for this phenomenon in the theories of socialism or the transitional society. There is a third hypothesis which has recently become very popular in the West: the theory that Soviet-type societies are the result of an attempt to institute socialism and bear the marks of this historical experience, but are in fact simply a version of the capitalist socio-economic formation. But the question then is, why are there no points in common between the ideologies of these oppositions and those of anti-capitalist movements in the West?

At this point usually another so-called explanation comes in: that these dissident movements in Eastern Europe and especially in the USSR are isolated intellectual movements which have no contact with the broad social strata most seriously affected by the reproduction of capitalist structures, especially the working class. But this is rather a reproach or, if it strives for the status of an "explanation", then itself still needs explaining. And on this point the scheme in which the structural characteristics of Western capitalism are generalised falls down completely. In capitalist societies, the intelligentsia is only a heterogeneous mass in a field of action dominated by the two basic classes; it does not appear as an independent force in social conflicts, but is divided between the two poles. In Soviet-type society (which is built of quite different elements from those in capitalism, so its ruling class evidently could not be described as bourgeois), on the other hand, class structure lies within the confines of an institutional system which by its very nature prevents social classes from becoming an independent political force, that is to say, from seeing themselves as particular classes in terms of an articulate ideology and from setting up specific organisations to advance their interests.

One could ask why the Soviet intelligentsia has not made contact with the working class, but that is not the right question. The question which in fact corresponds to the situation in Soviet-type societies is as follows: why is the intelligentsia – which does not constitute an autonomous class – able to create its own ideology and its own culture, and even its own counter-culture and embryonic counter-institutions, while the basic classes are unable even in this very restricted sense to form themselves into a class as a practical entity?

Which intelligentsia?

Once we begin to discuss the intelligentsia, we cannot avoid the question, which intelligentsia? If we were to accept, for the sake of neatness, the concept of the intelligentsia which is used by academic sovietologists and by the official Soviet sociologists in their pursuit of empirical enquiry, the results would be somewhat bizarre. Their definition is based on the criterion of vocational training, which can be easily processed as empirical data: an intellectual is someone who has a university or higher education diploma. Hence the inevitable conclusion that the intelligentsia is gradually integrated into the strata in power, and that dissidence is simply a deviation from normal behaviour.

And we get no further if we define the intelligentsia as a smaller group whose members do intellectual work without taking part in the execution of management and organisational tasks. In this sense, a teacher of literature is evidently an intellectual even if he has long since stopped following developments in the national literature; so too is the doctor who has a routine practice and does not interest himself in the progress of medical science. While this definition eliminates from the "intelligentsia" those people who are increasingly integrated into the power élite, it does not define a specific group from the point of view of the question with which we began this section, any more than (let us say) the skilled workers could be defined in such a way.

The social group which is capable of forming an autonomous ideology is the sub-group of intellectual workers whose members are in regular contact with the process of cultural and scientific creation. "Regular contact" does not mean "creation". The intellectual does not have to be a "creator" himself (the term is not only very limited, it is also extremely ambiguous), but he has actively to follow personal and written communications about scientific research and the production of cultural values. It is this institutionalised communication, within the limits of science and culture, that forms the public sphere, serving as a functional substitute for political discussion and organisation among those who take part in it.

Everybody knows how illusory the autonomy of the scientific and cultural community has become, not only in the Soviet-type societies, but in the capitalist West as well. The times when the so-called "free" intelligentsia formed the greatest part of the intelligentsia have passed. The free intellectual used to have financial resources unconnected with his professional activities or, if he did not, it was not his labour-power he sold but the product of his labour. Traditional organisations like the classical type of university were not employers in the modern sense; after the discharge of certain minimal requirements, the employees were to a large extent free. There was much less specialisation and hierarchisation than nowadays; non-authoritarian communication among intellectuals was not yet counteracted by anything other than traditional distinctions of rank and voluntary deference, and the hierarchisation of organisational roles had not yet taken place. But by the middle of this century the free intelligentsia had become a minority even in the sphere of social science and of humanist culture in the strictest sense. In Soviet-type societies this process has been even more vigorously intense than it has been under capitalism. Private incomes and assistance from non-official organisations have practically disappeared as sources of income. Organisations of intellectual labour have been subordinated to the hierarchy which embraces society as a whole, and have lost their autonomy to an even greater extent than their Western counterparts. The market in scientific and cultural products has been subjected to a central administrative management.

All this has tended to restrict the intelligentsia's ability to be a maker of public opinion, let alone a source of autonomous ideologies. This has been reinforced by a shift in the cultural basis of intellectual labour, i.e. the rise in the relative importance of a specialised scientific culture at the expense of the traditional humanist one. Social values are given less consideration in the motives for research. There are ever more researchers whose intellectual horizon does not extend beyond the verification and instrumentalist application of theories that have already been made. That part of intellectual production which is still aimed at "direct consumption" by the general public is falling, while there is a rise in the part which is directed towards "productive consumption", i.e. accumulation within mental production. And there is an ever-increasing specialisation even within the sphere of mental labour, whose products are used by increasingly differentiated disciplines. These tendencies are stronger in Soviet-type societies, since the effects of the factory-style organisation of research have been complemented by the intervention of administrative power in the discussion of problems which have an ideological connotation. Hence the flight of even serious researchers towards ideologically neutral topics, even when the division and organisation of intellectual labour in itself would not discourage them from ideological thinking.

And yet, if we look into these very adverse conditions in a more concrete manner, we realise more and more that even within the framework of hierarchically organised and administratively controlled culture and scientific life, various groups of the intelligentsia are still capable of forming and maintaining a relatively high-level social group consciousness. However wide the gap between the general public sphere and academic research, a minimum of public communication within the academic community is still an irreducible precondition of advancement in learning. Bureaucratic control may be so severe as to halt completely the development of whole sub-disciplines, but a modern society geared towards industrial growth and military competitiveness, and the Soviet-type society is beyond doubt such a society, cannot afford to block the advancement of all the sciences at the same time. If the censorship of those cultural products directed towards the wider public sphere is very strict, then the solution is an administratively created formal barrier between the general public sphere and the inner public sphere of the academic community. In this way they can maintain a relatively free flow of information inside the academic community which facilitates the formation of a professional consensus, without interfering with the bureaucratic manipulation of the public of the whole country. It is a common feature of all East European countries that they treat a good deal of this academic communication as state secrets, even if these do not represent a security risk from the point of view of military or industrial espionage. And even inside these formal barriers there are degrees of bureaucratic control: for example, criteria of censorship are much less severe for scholarly publications than for intellectual products aimed at a wider audience. And however hierarchical these research institutes are, somehow at least in principle they have to secure equality for discussants in scientific debates within the academic public sphere. And what is more, they have to give way to an extent to institutional relationships between scholars, even if these cut across their own hierarchical organisational structure (e.g. regular professional seminars, schools around leading academic personalities, etc.).

The same symptoms appear, though to a lesser extent, and with the due modifications, in the sphere of cultural production, which is aimed at direct consumption by the broad public. The national literature would be eradicated without the interaction between particular works. One book takes up the themes and motifs of another – in a polemicising or in a critical tone – then a piece of literary criticism deals with both; another piece, perhaps dealing with a third work, makes a hidden and polemical reference to the first piece of criticism, etc. Literary life presupposes the existence of regular personal communications, though it does not necessarily have to be institutionalised to the same degree as in the academic community – it can be maintained through loose friendships as well. This is true even of ideological utterances in the strict sense, which cannot afford to be absolutely repetitive, and even of political journalism, and the web of mutual responses and references resists all attempts to destroy it. Of course the rulers, in their desire to eliminate unwanted gaps, can gradually enlarge the range of taboos. But all they succeed in doing is to lower the public's threshold of receptivity to any emerging ideological differences. When independent political opinions are suppressed, it is aesthetic value judgments, abstract problems of philosophy and social theory and the evaluation of the remote historical past which assume political significance. And far from suppressing undesirable ideological differences, the perpetual extension of prohibitions often becomes counter-productive and leads to the crystallisation of political differences, since deviations are "discovered" where there is in fact only conformism and submission on the part of the authors concerned.

Of course, making incomplete allegorical references or indirect allusions is not the same thing as having an open confrontation between different ideological positions. But in the context of Soviet-type society even this reduced form of ideological reflection appears as a privilege for intellectuals, if we compare them with the basic classes of society. The basic classes are of course conscious of their identity. Consciousness of class identity is probably even clearer among the basic classes of Soviet-type society than in advanced capitalist society. The reason is simple: the demarcation line between classes quite visibly corresponds to the primordial distinction in the all-embracing institutional organisation of society, the distinction between those who have control over the activity of others and those who lack this control. (As regards this division of the social structure and particularly their own place in it, the intellectuals have a less clear collective consciousness than the basic classes, and their position has a relatively vague image in the consciousness of the two basic classes.) However, this class consciousness does not go beyond the level of a primitive "us and them" distinction. This kind of distinction, because of its non-differentiated character, can only be used to orient social behaviour among the interest relations of the groups concerned in the workplace and the living area, where all that is needed to decide who belongs to "us" and who belongs to "them" is to interpret the typical activities and material symbols (clothes, etc.). On a broader scale, this turns out to be an empty interpretative framework without practical consequences in any situation other than the extremely rare cases of mass riots, which are quickly crushed. In order to reach a point where there is solidarity and extensive co-operation, in order to realise an overall social programme, the classes need to institute their own political and economic organisations. But in Soviet-type society, none of the social classes is in a position to organise itself, not even the ruling class, although this does not mean to say that this class does not have a greater cohesion than the class it rules over. But the intelligentsia is in a privileged position compared with the basic classes. Because of the irreducible prerequisites of mental labour in the humanities and the sciences, the intelligentsia has, if not independent political organisations, then at least a functional equivalent to them. The relatively broad extent of academic communication (which certainly surpasses that of the basic groups) enables ideological and political allusions within the limits of the régime's ideological tolerance to be encoded and decoded regularly. The ideas which emerge from these decoded signals are, for the intelligentsia, the equivalent of a relatively high-level social ideology. Hence the phenomenon — which often seems so bizarre to Western eyes — of the authorities ruthlessly persecuting certain cultural or scientific expressions which seem to be completely innocent to judge from their direct content, but which nevertheless keep surging up and defying repression.

A *feature of post-stalinist society*

Even if the basic class consciousness is retarded at the level of a primitive "us and them" reflex, the general institutional set-up of scientific and cultural production invests the intelligentsia with the ability to form a collective consciousness of a relatively high level. But the simple existence of this set-up in itself explains nothing more than that. It does not explain the fact that the reproductive process of science and culture produces nonconformist intellectuals who, rejecting the official channels of communication reserved for the intelligentsia, try to work out ideas which by their very nature require a "counter-public sphere", so to speak. Nor do these general conditions of intellectual production explain the emergence of a sub-culture, providing nonconformism with a breathing space. The appearance of these two very specific and historically very easily definable phenomena is the product of the latter half of the 1960s.

During the classic period of stalinism, even the most elementary conditions for intellectual production barely survived. The dual (physical and ideological) terror did not even spare natural science. By establishing a symbolic relation between the smallest details of individual behaviour and the broadest objectives of social development, the official ideology made any lack of conformity with the expected behaviour appear to involve opposition to the ultimate aims, a political crime which demanded terror as a response. This is how suspicion became attached to the expert's estimation of technical possibilities and even to the objectivity of natural science itself. Because scientific and technical research were still considered essential the terror apparatus was not allowed to destroy their relative autonomy completely. Yet there was not a single discipline that was untouched by the political consequences of its inability to fulfil unrealisable demands. Agronomy and even the greater part of biology were colonised by a clique of charlatans who promised miracles by referring to quotations from Engels. Mathematical logic and cybernetics were denounced as bourgeois pseudosciences; and although modern theoretical physics was saved, this was only because of the military importance of its applications. In traditional social science, those branches of it that were less suited to serving the official ideology were artificially stunted, while those branches which were more useful for the aims of ideological propaganda, like history, were converted from a research subject into the production of political ideology. Towards the end of the stalinist era, economics no longer existed, other than as a set of administrative and accounting techniques and as material for teaching on political courses. Sociology was not able to form at all.

The activity in the sphere of the production of ideology was all the greater, at least according to the crude index of total output: the print-runs of books and other printed material, the numbers of visitors to concerts, exhibitions, etc. Yet this gave the intelligentsia little work to do. The apparatus of ideological control steered clear of uncertainties, and only allowed an extremely crude kind of mass production – huge series but offering little choice. Those members of the intelligentsia who were involved with producing these "types" were a restricted layer, corporately organised and highly privileged.

On the other hand, the ruling power also had an interest in

allowing a certain minimum variety to subsist, since this was indispensable for the occasional rites of exorcism. The earthquakes of forced industrialisation often imposed the need to change the previous "line"; they were as frequent as the changes of direction in foreign policy which resulted from the instability of the USSR's international situation. However, the continuity of the system presupposed the maintenance of the ideological fiction that the line of the moment embodied the sole policy that was compatible with the final aims of socialism. The most natural method of resolving this disharmony was to make it appear as if the official policy did not change at all, it was just that it had earlier been deflected from its correct path by a "deviationist" group. In order to do so, all that one had to do was to choose from the ever-available stock of variations the one which could most easily be declared to be a deviation, and sacrifice it as a scapegoat on the altar of the fictional continuity of the official policy.

Under such circumstances, not one group of the intelligentsia could think of creating its own group ideology, one that would be distinguishable from the ideology dictated by the ruling élite. The margin for autonomous thought was no greater than that which was allowed to specialists in culture and science. The official ideologues usually did no more than define the "general line"; applying it to the particular problems of philosophy, the sciences, the arts and literature was the job of specialists. This gave them a restricted but real chance to give their own interpretation, within the limits of their specific field, to the directing principles which had been formulated at the summit of power. The extremely small number of intellectuals who in the darkest years of stalinism tried to defend their cultural and scientific values were restricted to the use of this highly ambiguous tactic. In accepting unreservedly the general slogans of the official ideology, they so to speak "deepened" them at the same time, when applying them to their own particular field. It was in this way that certain groups of the intelligentsia were able to turn various situations to their advantage: in psychology the Pavlovians, and at other times the supporters of the socio-historical theory of behaviour, and in the field of literary criticism, first the representatives of the avant-garde and the Proletkult, and later the representatives of theory of realism.

The successes which were achieved in the course of this double game were highly dubious. The designation of a new ideological line always meant the liquidation of this or that group of intellectuals who were held responsible for the old line, and anyone who wanted to turn the conjuncture to his advantage had to involve himself in the confrontation on the ruling élite's side. Since usually the victims themselves had been responsible during previous campaigns for the suppression of authentic cultural values, the intellectuals who joined the choir of denunciation had an easy moral excuse: at the level of appearances the general policy was faultless and the entire responsibility for the troubles rested solely on that clique of intellectuals which previously monopolised the execution of the official line. However, this tactic was all the more ambiguous inasmuch as the role was played with a clear conscience. For the "correction of errors" was carried out by the most brutal means of repression. And the victory was only temporary. It was usually the most exposed participants in the most recent campaign, whatever their reasons for involvement, who were most likely to fall victim to the next inevitable change in the line.

Far from enabling a cultural and ideological underground to be built, the stalinist system was incompatible even with the lasting crystallisation of intellectual currents that stayed within the limits of tolerance of the official policy. It was only the reforms which were very gradually introduced from the middle of the 1950s that created the conditions for this. To the extent that mass terror receded and economic growth began to occur in a balanced way, the mobilising functions of the official ideology slowly diminished. The active intervention of the official ideology became completely dysfunctional in the sphere of scientific research and technology. If the economic aims of research were not disputed by the intellectual, the solution of scientific problems necessary to achieve them could be left entirely to the professional groups. The requirements of the ideology were now entirely negative: not to challenge the supremacy of the official ideology, or rather to celebrate ritually (on rare occasions only) a willingness to submit to that ideology. The economic and organisational conditions of research also developed enormously. The numbers of the scientific and technical intelligentsia increased rapidly. The centre of gravity of research shifted from the traditional higher educational institutions to research organisations which were either autonomous or attached to industry. The hierarchy of these organisations, running parallel to the state hierarchy, guaranteed that there were some possibilities for intellectuals to ascend to the lower and middle layers of the ruling class.

In the sphere of the social sciences, which were closer to ideology, the transformations were less significant. The ideological prohibitions remained stricter, the positive requirements from the official ideology were often still in effect. The direction of the process, however, was the same: the traditional disciplines were rebuilt and the most elementary conditions for the development of modern disciplines were fulfilled, especially in mathematical economics and sociology. In the sphere of cultural production, a growing role was given to consumer demand. In an ever-increasing proportion a demand arose for cultural products which had only a loose connection with the official ideology. The tight and corporately organised group of privileged manufacturers was no longer able to fulfil the changed demand. A slow process took place in which culture and the social sciences were being assimilated into other spheres of mass cultural production.

At the beginning, this progress did not take place by means of an organic adaptive evolution of the existing institutional system. In almost all the East European countries, the ending of mass terror brought about a division in the political élite of the ruling class, between those who had been directly involved in the practice of terror and therefore put up stubborn resistance to the reforms, and those who represented the interest in the demobilisation of everyday life. Because the reformers wanted to force the first of these groups to give ground, they tried to denounce them openly as being responsible for the crimes of stalinism, by making these crimes public. In this power struggle the reform faction tried to channel the activities of the intelligentsia, who were in search of greater autonomy, to their own uses. They protected the literary works which exposed the stalinist atrocities, pamphlets criticising stalinist economic policy, etc. The cultural and scientific freedom which was thus achieved was of course very fragile. Since it had no foundation in institutionalised rights but only in *ad hoc* interventions on the part of the top leadership, it lasted only as long as the unity of the political élite (and of the ruling class as a whole) took to re-establish itself. But for a time, public discussion of social problems could go a long way, and this inevitably gave rise to illusory hopes about the meaning of what was happening. The majority of intellectuals were hoping that, once the power of the reform group had become stabilised, official protection for independent thought would become routine, and that ultimately the *ad hoc* interventions would be transformed into institutionalised guarantees. Hence for a transitional period the gap between those intellectuals whose aspirations did not go beyond an improvement of the intelligentsia's cultural and social position and demanded more consumption and a better way of life, and those whose demands presupposed a transformation in the basic institutional structure of régime, was not yet visible. The illusion was that a gradual, organic transition from the one to the other was possible. It was a characteristic sympton of this political climate that writing in manuscript form, which was already flourishing, was never opposed to the official literature. The circulation of typewritten copies was seen as a kind of pre-publication which would be followed by their being brought out by state publishing houses or in journals.

Once the division in the ruling class had been overcome (the definitive date for the East European countries as a whole, was the end of the 1960s), it was time for disillusion. The new élite in power will only tolerate autonomy to the extent that the unified hierarchical system of institutions is not threatened with disintegration. It is clear now that we are not heading towards the institutionalisation of cultural and scientific freedoms, and that public debates are no longer permitted to continue even at the level which they had reached during the years of destalinisation. But it is also clear that the reunification of the ruling class does not mean a return to stalinism. The central apparatus no longer underwrites its power with mass terror, suppressing all particular interests. The differentiation in the economy has gone too far, mass consumption is too strongly integrated in the equilibrium of the economy, and the ruling class itself has become too interested in the expansion of the consumer goods market for it to be possible to return to the outright neglect of the particular interests of the various social groups. Thus the apparatus recognises the existence of such interests, without, however, allowing the interested groups to represent them by means of autonomous organisations, or to consolidate them in institutionalised forms. Only out of the goodness of its heart does the apparatus grant any favours that may be obtained, and it is only by means of the diffuse pressure brought to bear on the apparatus that the conflicting interest groups extort compromises from each other. In the consolidated post-stalinist system, the political élite thus underwrites its power by monopolising the role of referee in the solution of social clashes, a solution which therefore always presupposes its direct intervention. Hence it is characteristic of post-stalinist society that its coherence is no longer based on repression alone, but also on the passive consensus of the various social strata.

This state of affairs is expressed with the greatest clarity in the relations between workers and enterprise managements. The constant intervention by the central apparatus ensures the continuous satisfaction of the minimum demands of the former for guaranteed employment and a gradual rise in wages, and at the same time defends the latter against claims which are in excess of this minimum. While on the one hand it prevents the economic managers from putting all the costs of economic growth on the backs of the working class, the central apparatus also prevents the workers from going on strike or from instituting their own factory-level, regional or industry-level organisations, by which they might co-ordinate their resistance to attempts to exploit them further. In short, it limits the freedom of action of enterprise directors confronted by their employees, but it also protects them against the discontent of the latter. For the working class, the constant intervention of the central authorities in economic life appears, nevertheless, as a measure whose positive aspect consists in the fact that it seems to prevent the economic managers from exploiting their position unscrupulously in order to maximise their level of consumption at the workers' expense.

The majority of intellectuals themselves also accept this new balance of power in the post-stalinist system. Like the workers and enterprise-level management, the intellectuals also have a positive interest in maintaining the central apparatus's mediation. If they renounce those freedoms which are incompatible with the survival of the unified ruling system, in exchange they get not only the comfort and status symbols of the intellectuals' way of life and consumer patterns, but even some very real cultural freedoms as well. They can continue with their creative activities within the limits laid down by the official taboos, and if they are skilful in manoeuvring they can even push back slightly the limits to their margins of action. And yet it is precisely this situation which produces the minority of intellectuals who depart consciously from the official institutional framework of culture and science. At first the "primitive accumulation" of nonconformism takes place: unless they fall rapidly in line, the leading intellectuals who used to attack stalinism under the protection of the supreme power find themselves marginalised. But this is only the first step; there comes a further accumulation which is based on post-stalinist society's own mechanisms.

The continuing ideological control of research in the natural sciences after the reform period is confined to ensuring that the negative norms are obeyed. But the political connections of research control and the social utilisation of scientific results cannot be hidden from the eyes of East European scientists. And in this respect they are subjected to strict positive norms. Increased professional autonomy encourages this or that expert to try and influence social decisions which concern his own speciality. The post-stalinist system produces but does not tolerate the type of expert who is well-known in Western society, who – conscious of his own scientific competence – intervenes in social questions with a great deal of naïvety but also with a great deal of courage.

Another permanent factor of marginalisation relates to international scientific contacts. Here again, we are not talking simply about the slowly decomposing rigidities of the old system, but also about the inherent limits of the new system. International contacts are constantly being extended, but the researchers have only very restricted opportunities to take part in them as individuals. Private travel still takes place on a strictly *ad hoc* basis, and permission to travel is only valid for a single occasion. And researchers are only allowed to maintain regular contacts as representatives of their official scientific organisation. However, the very rapid developments in key research sectors brings extremely great pressure to bear on the researchers who work in them to follow closely the new results which are achieved abroad. Anyone who does not want to be left behind must therefore at some time or another break the restrictions which stem from the monopoly character of the official organisation of science. This can result in punitive sanctions which in particularly serious cases go as far as marginalisation itself. The way to avoid this conflict is to choose a kind of internal marginalisation, by turning to areas in which international competition is not so strong. Researchers who make this choice often expend a decreasing amount of their creative energies in official research tasks and begin to wonder about specific social issues which concern their own current situation.

But though marginalising forces are regularly present in the natural sciences, their principal area of activity is the social sciences and cultural production. As far as research into the natural sciences is concerned, rising in the hierarchy of scientific organisation involves a greater freedom of choice in what problems to examine, and freer access to material resources. However, in the social sciences, which are in direct contact with ideological production, the correlation is far from being this unambiguous. Here, the higher up a person is in the official hierarchy, the more he is forced to make substantial concessions to the ruling ideology. The decomposition of classic stalinism as far as social science is concerned means the bare presence of certain themes for discussion and some cultural products available for a limited audience, in which one can avoid clashing with the official ideology. Scientific topics and artistic and literary genres which are peripheral from the ideological point of view can be adapted to the inclination of some intellectuals, but for others, simply choosing to stay in this sphere is internal marginalisation itself. Behind this choice unabsorbed energies are often hidden, seeking an outlet outside the official public sphere.

The manoeuvring between peripheral and central topics and genres has a particular generational aspect, which is quite apparent in the case of social science researchers but can also be demonstrated in artistic and literary life. At the beginning of his career, the young researcher takes his bearings chiefly according to the internal criteria of his profession. During his university and postgraduate studies, it is only the worthless elements that play a role in the quasi-political official organisations, only the deliberate careerists who try to brush up their scientific performance with the aid of the official ideology. At the lower levels of the hierarchy, one can still advance by showing competence in one's profession; it is more natural to choose problems which concern peripheral details, and the pressure to publish is less strong. But at the age of thirty or so, one encounters the necessity to choose. In order to continue rising the academic ladder, the researcher must orientate his thinking towards the central topics and intensify his publishing activity, and this makes it inevitable that he will make considerable ideological concessions and play an active political role. At this point, prudent nonconformists take the route towards internal marginalisation. The majority, on the other hand, try to make a rational compromise. But in order to do so, they need extraordinary ability and good luck. In most cases, the compromise leads either towards pure careerism, or to confrontation with the management apparatus and probably to marginalisation.

What makes it extremely difficult to manoeuvre is the competition between researchers who are not determined nonconformists but try to preserve their autonomy. Each of them wants to pay the lowest price possible for increasing his opportunities for research. But in doing so, he threatens to make the situation of the others worse, because he irritates the sensitivities of officialdom by his behaviour, which is not conformist enough. This is why the scientific community itself exercises strong pressure on its members to respect what is laid down by the official ideology. At the same time as claiming to defend the opportunities which have already been obtained in research and publication, the research intellectuals in social science censor each other themselves. Each researcher may fulfil the function of ideological control, at least in the form of an occasional criticism. The usual conflict between generations in the scientific community thus inevitably takes on a political character. And in this political conflict, nonconformist attitudes crystallise, or rather a considerable number of intellectuals find themselves pushed, in spite of themselves, into peripheral positions where they can no longer obtain substantial advantages simply by presenting that degree of conformism which they themselves are still ready to accept morally.

The "sub-intelligentsia"

Post-stalinist development reproduces the nonconformist intelligentsia on a regular basis but a phenomenon no less important is that at the same time it isolates them from the established intellectuals as a whole. For the majority of intellectuals, any action which breaks the accepted rules of the game from the inside represents a risk that they will lose the positions they have so far reached. The more often the demonstrations of nonconformism take place and the more brutally the repressive apparatus intervenes in the sphere of science and culture in order to isolate the established intelligentsia from the contagion of "deviant" ideas and attitudes, the more intense is the surveillance of personal contacts, and the greater the inherent risk of circulating manuscripts before their publication. All critical thought becomes suspect; bans on the public sphere are increased; it once again becomes quite difficult to bypass the official ideology. Of course, it would take a still more brutal intervention to stifle nonconformism as a social phenomenon. It would not be sufficient even to exercise systematic selective terror against people who are already nonconformists: preventive terror would be necessary, which would inevitably affect the whole of the intelligentsia. The intelligentsia is opposed, of course, to everything that tends or is assumed to tend towards the installation of preventive terror, and thus erects a screen over nonconformism as a social phenomenon, whether it wants to or not. But the intelligentsia would be quite happy if the pressure of public opinion by itself were able to eliminate nonconformism. The sole exception to this general rule is the group of younger-generation intellectuals who have not yet been faced with the obligatory choice: either to integrate themselves completely or to marginalise themselves completely.

The established intellectuals' slogans against nonconformism are extremely diverse, but all these different voices are only the various lines of a single polyphonic chorus of general rejection. The most moderate attitude is simply to blame the nonconformists' behaviour: "What they want is good, but they do it the wrong way. What's the use of provoking the authorities, the situation will only get worse." A few notes higher, we already hear the hypocritical questioning of the lack of purity in the scientific or literary character of the nonconformists: "We all know their work is worthless – if it wasn't for the political fuss, nobody would be paying any attention to it." The line above does not even sing about the content of the work, but about the psychology of the writers: "Of course, they must not be shut up in psychiatric asylums. But most of them are unbalanced and frustrated because of their lack of literary or scholarly success, and this nonconformism is a way of making up for it." Higher still, we can already hear open denunciation: "These people are intolerant. They are bigger enemies of cultural freedoms than the government itself." The top line sings the very same melody as the official propaganda: "But it's absolutely scandalous to have connections with the Western press; they are harming the international reputation of the socialist countries."

One might expect, with very good reason, that without finding contact with any other social group, the marginalised nonconformist intellectuals cannot survive. But the curious thing is that the intelligentsia of the post-stalinist period, by marginalising a small minority among its members, not only reproduces the phenomenon of nonconformism, but also reproduces the social group (as a by-product of its own development) that provides a natural environment for nonconformist individuals.

The expansion of factory-type research and cultural organisations, which was held back in the East European countries partly by their relative underdevelopment and partly by the inhibiting effects of stalinism, only took off during the destalinisation period, and succeeded in producing significant social effects towards the middle of the 1960s. Certain symptoms of this process have already been referred to above: the sharp increase in the strength of the scientific and technical intelligentsia, a shift in the centre of gravity of research from the university to independent research institutes or institutes attached to industry. As far as the social sciences are concerned, we are at the very beginnings of organised research in the modern sense. Similar phenomena occur also in the sphere of traditional humanist culture, under the influence of the growth in organisations of mass communication.

The factory-type organisation of scientific and cultural production goes beyond standardising intellectual labour that is subject to hierarchical relations, and gives birth also to auxiliary personnel: interviews, data-processing operators, archivists, translators, etc. This work is not always carried out by permanent employees; from the organisation's point of view, it can be more economical to make freelance contracts than to pay regularly a personnel whose services are subjected to seasonal interruptions. But this does not stop a quite considerable social group from finding an exclusive source of income from this work. We call the members of this group "sub-intellectuals", for want of a better term.

The incorporation of the sub-intelligentsia into the functioning of large-scale scientific and cultural industry first of all gives a certain material security to the nonconformist intellectuals. Removed from their jobs, they do not fall into a vacuum; on the peripheries of the intelligentsia there is a significant social group, and they can therefore assimilate its life-style without renouncing their intellectual existence. The repressive apparatus, of course, is still capable of preventing them from obtaining even auxiliary work of this kind. But in order to do so, it has to intervene on each particular occasion; and the more widespread the scientific and cultural industry becomes, the more difficult it is to control those marginal people who are looking for work. (Before the emergence of this factory-type culture quite the opposite was true: only direct intervention could secure a job for someone who was thrown out of his proper job.)

Still more important, perhaps, is the fact that the sub-intelligentsia guarantees the marginalised nonconformists an intellectual environment – people with whom to discuss. In fact the auxiliary services of large-scale cultural and scientific industry get hold of a large part of those individuals who, though they aspire to an intellectual career, have not succeeded in obtaining the appropriate degree or in finding a qualified job equal to their degree. For them this is still the nearest thing to being an intellectual, a kind of "second best" opinion. The attraction stems not so much from a wish to imitate the consumer habits of the intelligentsia (other sources of income would allow them to do so in the same way) as from the desire to maintain regular contact with intellectual activities and to be plugged into the communication channels of the intelligentsia. The work of an interviewer affords contact with sociological research, the work of a translator keeps him in touch with literature or with some field of social science, etc. Above all, among sub-intellectuals with degrees there are many who are not content with passively satisfying their curiosity, but try to have some autonomous scientific or cultural activity. Their chances of success in submitting their work to the consideration of the scientific community or in having it published in book form or in an official review are clearly much less than the chances of the established intellectuals. They therefore have a very strong motivation to look for a non-official public sphere and to find readers, critics, and people with whom to discuss among their own ranks. This is still true even if we have to admit that for a minority of them their position as sub-intellectuals is only a temporary one, and (the result of the rigid labour market) they are only delayed on their way to joining the intellectual establishment. The nonconformists thus find quite a receptive audience among the sub-intellectuals; it is relatively easy for them to direct their aspirations towards opposition — aspirations which, having no place in the established science and culture, seek fulfilment on their own, outside the official institutions anyway.

Samizdat

Towards the end of the 1960s, the social conditions for nonconformism were met in the majority of the East European countries. Almost everywhere, the new balance of power of post-stalinist society had consolidated; the limits of the freedoms concerning scientific research and cultural production had been delineated; the rules of behaviour within these limits had been defined; large-scale intellectual industry, together with its auxiliary services, had obtained the crucial size that enabled it to produce considerable social effects, including the necessary number of auxiliary jobs. On the fringes of the official culture, almost everywhere a non-official sub-culture had formed, maintained mainly by sub-intellectuals, and, to a lesser extent, by the younger part of the established intelligentsia. The production of nonconformism became regular, as did the marginalisation of nonconformist intellectuals into the sphere of sub-intellectuals; these people are responsible for the dynamisation of the sub-culture of the sub-intellectuals and for its transformation into an embryonic counter-culture. From this counter-culture has come the counter-public sphere of manuscripts which enable personal nonconformist attitudes to be objectivised in the form of social ideologies, and as a result the defence of cultural autonomy has been transformed into political opposition. But while nonconformism is a general phenomenon and in almost all East European countries develops parallel with the growth of scientific and cultural production, this latter phenomenon of samizdat seems for the moment to be unique. Only in one country (although this is the USSR, precisely the most important Soviet-type society for world history) does samizdat circulate on a large enough scale and regularly enough to warrant its description as a counter-public sphere. "For the moment," we said: and in fact the difference between nonconformism as a personal attitude and the counter-public sphere as a more or less institutionalised means of communication invites the interpretation that these two simultaneous cases are actually successive stages in an evolutionary sequence. If the evolutionary tendency as outlined really exists, then we are entitled to see the present of the Soviet underground as the future of the underground in the other countries of Eastern Europe.

However, there is nothing that enables us to state that post-stalinist development is generally speaking more advanced in the USSR than it is elsewhere. The USSR is, in fact, ahead of the others in certain respects, for example in the growth of large-scale scientific industry. In other respects, however, the other East European countries are more advanced: East Germany, Czechoslovakia and Hungary in individual consumption, Poland and Hungary in de-ideologisation of culture, Hungary in the decentralisation of the economic management system. Rather than simply representing the future of the other East European countries, the USSR represents a unique combination of advanced and retarded sectors. We can easily understand that it is not post-stalinist progress which alone explains the formation of samizdat, but also the extraordinary rigidity of the official media, the unique interpenetration of the administration of science and culture with terror organisations, etc. It would therefore be false to extrapolate automatically the birth of a samizdat counter-public sphere in the rest of the East European countries. What we can say is that there is the possibility of a repetition of the coincidence of the results of uneven development and of some historical circumstances, a coincidence favourable to the formation of non-official means of circulation. We may add to this the fact that the regularisation of post-stalinist development is probably increasing everywhere the chances of this kind of "happy" coincidence of sociological conditions.

But even if the Russian underground with its articulated ideologies and embryonic movements remains a unique phenomenon, this does not make it less true that its basis is the general post-stalinist development. We thus have every right to apply to it the explanatory scheme which we have presented up to this point; all we have to do is pay attention that we do not deduce more than really follows from it. For example, the particular physiognomy of the Russian oppositional ideologies obviously does not follow from it. These reflect the common action of the spiritual traditions of pre-revolutionary Russia, the unparalleled discontinuity of the culture of the Russian intelligentsia, and the almost complete isolation of this latter from the intellectual developments in the West over the last fifty years; they also reflect the unrivalled moral prostitution of contemporary Russian society, etc. But for an understanding of how the Russian nonconformist intelligentsia makes its choice from among these intellectual hesitations, the general explanatory framework for the interpretation of post-stalinist society can play a key role. And it is absolutely vital for discovering the sociological functions of the ideologies which form within the counter-public sphere.

What is the role of the counter-public sphere in Soviet-type society? Whose ideologues are the writers, journalists and philosophers in the underground? If we accept the above-mentioned general explanatory scheme, then the answer is that among the important social groups there is not one whose interests find their representation in these people's activities. No doubt they are closest to the sub-intellectuals. However, these do not constitute a self-sufficient social group; they are dependent on the intelligentsia, both in the social division of labour and in culture. It is the expansion of organised scientific and cultural production which determines the expansion of the tasks carried out by the sub-intellectuals, and it is from the established intellectuals that they take the greater part of their culture. Hence their inability to become the subjects of an independent ideology.

Still less can we describe as an autonomous social group the younger generation of the intelligentsia which has not yet arrived at the point where it must choose between integration and marginalisation. This group is loose and unstable: part of it, the smaller part, gravitates towards the sub-intelligentsia, while the greater part gravitates towards the higher levels of the hierarchy of intellectual labour.

As far as the established intelligentsia itself is concerned, its attitude towards the underground is, to say the least, ambiguous. If we set aside the conscious careerists, all intellectuals go through the experiences of frustration which lead the nonconformists deliberately to choose marginalisation. For every writer, it is an abnegation to admit that because the canons of socialist realism have become less strict, this still does not mean that there is freedom of creation. Every sociologist, economist and historian meets insurmountable barriers as soon as he enters a sphere which is "delicate" from the standpoint of the official ideology or when he tries to make independent generalisations which are impossible to camouflage with the phrases of that ideology. Every researcher in natural sciences submits to the administrative constraints which restrict communication among scientists. And in general, every intellectual experiences the frustration caused by the lack of information, while everyone at least once in his life has to undergo the shame of being forced to identify in public with ideas which he mentions only with contempt and irony in private. However, as we have seen, the established intelligentsia has no interest in seeing this *éducation sentimentale* lead to nonconformism on a massive scale. Even if indirectly it provides a shelter for nonconformist intellectuals, its direct attitude towards them is none the less hostile. It does not recognise itself in ideological utterances which put a question mark over the whole present institutional framework of society.

And the working class? In contrast to the intellectuals, the workers have no interest in the elimination of the underground. But nor do they have any interest in its survival. The question does not even pose itself for the working class. The nonconformist counter-culture forms in the sphere of communication between intellectuals; it is an irreducible epiphenomenon of intellectual work, and inevitably establishes a connection among all those who conform to the intelligentsia's subculture and way of life. The workers do not have access to this. It is not simply that contacts along the class frontiers are in any case less frequent. Even among themselves, the members of the working class are not linked by a network of communication comparable to that which makes the intelligentsia a coherent cultural entity and which serves as the basis for the circulation of samizdat. This kind of communication is not a natural part of the lifestyle of the worker. To establish an opening through which the underground can communicate with the workers, the workers themselves must reach the stage of organised class struggle and institute, at least at factory level, associations which can then be stabilised. Then these organisations would be able to interact with the underground. But in Soviet-type societies, the working class is as incapable of organising itself as any other social group. While the rare moments of cataclysmic crisis in the system give rise to strike committees and workers' councils, these organisational results of popular uprisings never succeed in consolidating after normal reproduction has been re-established. In such circumstances, to a working class which is deprived of its organisations, the ideas of the underground are not social facts, or else they are the particular business of an alien group. (What is more, it considers the members of this group generally to belong among the privileged consumers of the surplus product. This sometimes allows the manipulators of the mass media to transform neutrality into active resentment: "They live on what we produce and they're still not satisfied! It's because they're after even more, to our disadvantage.")

But if the underground is necessarily isolated from the large groups of society, is it not true that the sole function of the oppositional ideologies is to talk to the nonconformist intellectuals themselves, to give them moral justification and hope to hold out? Should we not draw the conclusion that the counter-public sphere only serves one social aim, which is to preserve itself? If it is the case, then inevitably the judgement of the established intelligentsia must be accepted willy-nilly: the underground does harm rather than good to the cause of cultural and social freedom. The most one can do, then, to separate oneself from the repulsive anti-nonconformist chorus, is to attest to a certain sociological understanding by observing that nonconformism, reproduced by social causes, cannot be made to vanish by exorcism.

And yet this line of reasoning is begging the question, and belies the secret wishes of the reasoner. It is quite true: the counter-public sphere simply cannot be a tool for political propaganda, if we understand by propaganda the rationalisation of the radical interests of a class, that is, interests which are tied to the radical transformation of the existing institutional order. But even in this very broad sense, political propaganda is not the only way of influencing the society's consciousness. There is also another form, which is more diffuse in its effects but no less real: we could call it propaganda by action. Populist terrorism in the nineteenth century entered into this category, as well as the activities of the ideologues of the counter-public sphere in our times.

Propaganda by action means setting an example, showing by one's own actions that it is not necessary to accept the world installed by the régime, that it is possible to act according to norms other than those of the existing institutional system. In societies where the dominated class has the means to create autonomous organisations, no particular significance is attached to this form of propaganda; generally speaking, it does not constitute a separate task but is an integral part of the normal functioning of the class organisations and the everyday life of their members. Its importance is so much the greater in a society in which no one social class is in a position to organise itself, especially when the institutional system manages not only to impose its supremacy externally on all classes but also the models of behaviour and attitudes compatible with its reproduction. We are not saying, of course, that the cohesion of the system is ensured only or principally by a belief in the impossibility of change: it is ensured in the first place by institutional mechanisms and by institutionalised interests. However, this belief plays its part in ensuring the system's coherence. Consequently the counter-public sphere, as well as nonconformism as a mode of personal behaviour, decrease the coherence of the system, by their very existence. And not only by this. The samizdat literature breaks the monopoly of the ruling ideology's patterns of thought, and introduces new concepts and alternative ideas into the social consciousness. Even the most ancient and reactionary myths have a clearly positive role from this point of view, since they in fact multiply the number of patterns of thought which can be confronted with each other. The greater the diversity of the ideologies formed in the underground, the more differentiated social thinking becomes, and the easier it is to relativise the official ideology's *Weltanschauung*.

Another consequence of the formation of a counter-public sphere is that it creates a sphere in which there are real social and philosophical debates. Whoever chooses the underground to make his ideas public will not be looking for adroit compromise, nor will he dodge the uncomfortable consequences of his position in order to make himself acceptable to the authorities; rather, he forces himself to draw all his conclusions and to confront the rival ideologies with them. Of course one of the concomitants of the underground's isolation, an almost inevitable one, is that rational discussion is sometimes replaced by blind sectarian struggle. What also happens is that the nonconformist ideologies only create the illusion of autonomous thought. The intellectual traditions are so poor that the nonconformist intellectuals are forced to draw from the official ideology from time to time: they try to make themselves an image of idealism on the basis of manuals on "dialectical materialism", to work out the essence of trotskyism or populism on the basis of manuals on "scientific socialism". Instead of creating true conceptual alternatives, they thus simply give real life to the phantom enemies of the official manuals. And yet it cannot be disputed that the total effect of the intellectual production which goes on in the counter-public sphere is liberating.

It is practically impossible to say how deep this effect is. However, what we do know is that it spreads in the first place to the subintellectuals and to the younger generation of the intelligentsia. But beyond this, we know practically nothing. How many readers has samizdat? How many people do not read it but are informed about it by means of personal communication? How many people are capable of deciphering the allusions made to the ideas from the manuscript literature that appear from time to time in the official press? We know the answers to none of these questions. And even if the answer were given, we would still know only very little. For the hold which the underground ideologies have on the thinking of those whom they affect depends to a great extent on non-ideological factors. It depends on the nature of the internal changes in the institutional development of Soviet-type societies, and on the nature of the changes in its external environment to which this development must accommodate itself. And all this – the systematic changes themselves and, with even greater reason, the external effects – can only be very faintly predicted.

Before the first Russian revolution, no one was capable of telling how deeply the wound made by the populist terrorism of the 1880s had affected the belief in the sanctity and inviolability of the autocracy. Today, it is no easier to appreciate the impression left on social consciousness by nonconformism and its more objectified, organised manifestations, the counter-public sphere of the samizdat. But whether it is a strong or weak one, at present it is the only terrain in the East European countries where on a mass scale (and not simply for certain randomly marginalised individuals) the following problem is posed: whether to be integrated in the system or to oppose it, whether to make minor repairs to given institutions or to create counter-institutions. And the choice of the marxists cannot be in doubt.

The various trends

As far as the most abstract practical decision is concerned, then, our proposition does not differ from that of the Western left: one must have solidarity with everyone in the Soviet-type societies who disputes their institutions. But when one starts to make the content of the choice more precise, the differences come into the foreground. The explanatory scheme outlined in this chapter has a series of specific consequences which give the idea of solidarity a different meaning from that which it usually has.

First of all, we are now in a position to interpret in their own social context those ideological manifestations which do not fail to shock the Western left. We can understand now that the growing popularity of programmes for moral regeneration and cultural renaissance as alternatives to political action is closely related to the limitations of the underground's practical opportunities. We may point out that the dreadful conservatism of Russian national messianism is nothing but a reaction to the social isolation of the nonconformist intelligentsia. It "explains" the indifference of the masses towards the concerns of the intellectuals; the decomposition of the holy trinity of patriarchal folk life, orthodox religion and autocracy has led to a general relativisation of values, an ethical nihilism. It also tells the intellectuals that their cultural and moral movements can in themselves save the nation, since, if the rebirth of the national consciousness takes place, the re-establishment of the old order of values and the former organic unity between the educated élite and the people, etc., will be automatic. We can understand how the uncritical enthusiasm which the Russian liberals show for Western liberalism reflects less a lack of information (the traditionalists who reject democracy *en bloc* as an institutional system that corrupts the life of the folk are no better informed) than the fact that liberalism does not appear on the horizon of the Russian intellectuals as an economic and political mechanism but as a set of "inalienable" human rights. It is not ideological naïvety that leads marxists who put their hope in "leninist norms" to expect the reforms to come from above, but the fact that in Soviet-type society the only social force which is capable of acting — the only force to which it is not absurd *ab ovo* to address a programme of action — is the state itself. After all, it is not only the marxist leninists who, on emerging from the shadows of the underground, begin all of a sudden to give advice to the political leaders. And we can understand, too, how those people, such as the Russian orthodox "personalists" who reject the conservative myth of the Russian national essence and also reject any collaboration with the régime, are inclined to look outside society, in the sphere of religious transcendence, for a basis for ideas of personal freedom and moral autonomy.

In the second place, we can justify the necessity for solidarity with nonconformism not only in moral terms, but in political ones as well. The East European established intellectuals love to congratulate themselves on the part they play in defending democratic thought against this or that oppositional current. Who has not heard those hypocritical declarations which are so often made in "progressive" Russian circles, rejecting national messianism by accusing it of seeking to put the Russian people back into the irons of the traditional institutions of the patriarchal monarchic state? One does not get very far by answering such arguments with the remark that yes, it's true the content of the opposition's nationalism is scandalous, but there is also a heroic gesture involved in the act of daring to flaunt these scandalous ideas in the faces of the régime, etc. But it is not necessary to confine oneself to this empty moralising. For every oppositional ideology, if it is really oppositional, if it does in fact transcend the official framework of communication and social discussion, implies a deep democratic content, even if its explicit statements are directly anti-democratic. Those people who only seek to enlarge and loosen up the official institutions from inside, and who fear the provocations of the nonconformists because they endanger those liberties which have already been obtained, are simply defending the intellectuals' privileges. Their concern is to preserve and extend those prerogatives which in a society that has no proper public sphere are attached to the public sphere in science and culture. On the other hand, those people who leave the official framework of intellectual production in order to create a non-official independent public sphere are thereby challenging the institutional system itself, in which access to the public sphere is a privilege that depends on one's position in the social division of labour and one's educational qualifications. They cannot profess such an utterly anti-democratic doctrine that it would prevent them from serving the cause of the democratisation of the public sphere.

Yet although solidarity is due to the nonconformist intellectual movements, against the defenders of the status quo, it does not follow that all these movements are of equal value. Nevertheless, the third consequence of the explanatory scheme outlined in this chapter is that we shall distinguish them from each other according to different criteria from those which apply to the Western anti-capitalist movements. We shall not judge the various oppositional ideologies by criteria which have no practical meaning for them. We shall not expect the latter to be able to build up connections with the working class or to prepare the ground for organised class movements. On the other hand, we shall expect them to do everything within the limits of their ability to dispel the belief in the necessity or indispensability of the existing institutional system. We shall expect them not to exclude from the nonconformist community, on religious, national, racial or other grounds, any individuals who choose marginalisation. It is with such criteria as a basis that one can criticise the followers of Russian national messianism who, in referring to the interests of the Russian state, are ready to take part in the nationalist games of the ruling power or, worse, to help its attempts to obtain an active mass base by stirring up the lowest kinds of hatred against racial or national minorities. It is with such criteria as a basis that one can also criticise those marxist leninists for whom marxism means continuity with the official ideology and are hoping for reforms from above.

These insights alone do not make it possible to inaugurate a dialogue with the various movements of the nonconformist intellectuals in the USSR. But if such a dialogue is possible at all, then it must be conducted according to the principles outlined above.

4 The Two Systems in Action

The idea of the convergence of the two world systems is almost as old as their coexistence. Of the numerous versions of this theory, that of "industrial society" is the most widespread. In the heroic age of large-scale machine industry (so the theory runs), primitive technology did not yet unambiguously determine the social organisation of production. At the beginnings of the development of contemporary "industrial society", therefore, differences which were historical in origin could play a significant role in the organisation of society. Where the industrial revolution took place within the context of private enterprise, capitalism evolved; where it took place on the basis of state ownership of the means of production, socialism evolved. But when technical development reaches the stage at which it is based on science, the differences between the respective points of departure lose their significance. Modern technology leaves no freedom of choice for the social patterns of the division of labour and co-operation. It directly defines the appropriate labour process and, through this, defines the wider social relations as well. In every mature industrial society there is the same technical division of labour, the same pattern of consumption, stratification and social mobility; the relation between the economy and politics is the same; and most important, specialised technical and scientific knowledge play the same role in the administration of social processes.

These prophets of industrial society were not motivated by the similarity of observable characteristics in the two systems. They were, in reality, interested in an ideological justification of Western capitalism. They wanted to prove that modern capitalism was no longer capitalism but, from the class point of view, a neutral industrial society, that it was not the interests of the bourgeoisie which governed social processes but the requirements of technological and economic rationality. Like every social theory which also functions as an ideology, the theory of industrial society owed its powers of persuasion primarily to the fact that what it said corresponded to beliefs which were regularly reproduced in many walks of everyday life. As a theory it did not stand up well to examination. Most of its predictions were not precise enough to be verified experimentally, and those which were did not stand up to the test of experience. But this did not damage their popularity, so long as they could fulfil their ideological function unhindered. However, when the cultural, social, ecological and finally the economic disruptions of "welfare capitalism" buried a significant portion of the everyday beliefs that made up the background of the theory, the theory itself immediately became problematical too. The ideological movements thrown up by these disruptions rejected one-sided technological determinism and put in doubt the idea that technology might be the neutral tool of any social aims. For them modern technology has become the tool of oppression. With its extreme separation of mental and manual labour and its connection of the labour-process to large, hierarchical organisations, it subjugates the worker as producer. With its increasingly perfect manipulation of the masses, on the other hand, it oppresses him as a consumer. It is not the so-called purely objective requirements of technical development which determine the development of social organisation but the social consequences of class rule which determine technological development.

The idea of the convergence of the two systems was not affected by this critique. On the contrary, the notion of convergence was beginning to penetrate left-wing social science (including the marxism which was then freeing itself from the successor parties of the Comintern), at the point when the latter, with its own critical technological conception, was in the process of undermining theoretically the very basis of the convergence thesis. As far as empirical facts are concerned, even the marxists now accept the predictions of the theory of industrial society: the trends of technological development in the two societies are becoming more and more parallel, and consequently the similarity is ever greater in the field of the division of labour and the pattern of consumption, and it is becoming increasingly clear that real social power in both societies is being transferred into the hands of some sort of technocracy. The only difference is that, in keeping with the different structure of the explanation, the theories of the left do not conclude that neither system is capitalist any longer, but rather that both are.

The left-wing version of the convergence theory voices the related disillusionment that the East European experiment has not led to socialism. Its function is to finally rid Western intellectuals of their illusions about Soviet-type societies. In consequence, what it has to say is purely negative: if the Soviet model is followed, it is impossible to stop those tendencies which are the targets of left-wing social criticism. And for this, in fact, it is enough to show that the behaviour of East European societies in relation to the tendencies criticised is increasingly similar to the behaviour of modern capitalism. For the left wing of Eastern Europe, however, the question emerges in a different context. For us the question is not simply the ways in which the two systems are similar. The most important question is the very one of how they differ. Soviet-type societies are also class societies, in the full sense of the word, but the methods of class rule and the chances of organised class struggle are quite different here from what they are under capitalism. The dynamic of economic cycles and their political after-effects are fundamentally different. Differences which cannot be ignored cut across the undoubted similarities in the hierarchical division of labour. A marxist theory that seeks to justify its existence in Eastern Europe cannot ignore these differences. What is more, we cannot have the same relation as the Western left even towards phenomena which really are similar. We cannot be satisfied with the conclusion that the structure of Soviet-type societies does not exclude the reproduction of the phenomena criticised — for example, the pattern of consumption and the technostructure characteristic of modern capitalism. We must also examine what sorts of mechanisms reproduce them, for the "same" phenomena are not the same from the standpoint of social praxis if different mechanisms are producing them.

The left-wing convergence theory does not state that there are no differences in the social, institutional and class structure of the two societies. The theory's adherents argue that these differences are inconsequential, since they do not have significant results in the observable behaviour of the two systems. Thus the procedure for a critique of the theory should be as follows. As a first step, a socio-economic model of the two societies should be worked out. Then the behavioural regularities, both different and similar (though developed under the influence of different causes), should be deduced from the two models. If we succeed in deducing the similarities mentioned by the left-wing convergence theory from this particular model, then this gives us an explanation for something the convergence theory only describes. If we also succeed in deducing systematic differences from this particular model and the deductions from this model can also be verified empirically, then we can also use the model for other phenomena which contradict the convergence theory.

The aim of this chapter is more modest than this. It does not attempt a systematic elaboration of these models, but merely tries to establish some very important differences in the fields of economic organisation and class structure. We cannot therefore provide strict deductions about the behavioural regularities of the two systems. We must content ourselves with a short discussion of behavioural regularities in the light of the distinctions indicated. At most this will make these theoretical distinctions plausible. But, as a beginning, this is perhaps something, especially if we consider that with the help of models sketched in this way we can succeed in showing significant differences among the very phenomena which the marxist convergence thesis is fond of quoting.

Our approach will be to bring into the model only those differences which are not the subject of debate among marxists. Furthermore, we shall only consider general differences in the models. That is, we shall set aside differences which are associated with initial historical conditions, the socio-economic backwardness of Soviet-type societies, the world economic and political background of the original process of accumulation in the Soviet Union, etc. Thus we shall handle our model as if there were no difference in the point of departure. This abstraction narrows still further the group of social processes that we can explain, but as a first step it seems expedient to do it. In this way, we can get round the danger of trying to explain by means of our model those differences which in reality result from differences of historical circumstance and not from the peculiarities of the systems.

The structural differences that we are going to consider are all related to the following very orthodox assertion: under capitalism it is the private ownership of the means of production that is dominant, whereas in Soviet-type societies the means of production are under state ownership. By "the domination of private property" we mean that rights to a share in the surplus product are bought and sold on the capital market; that shareholders can influence the use to which their capital is put, at least in so far as they can withdraw their capital from one enterprise and invest it in another; that the shares of a section of the enterprises are either entirely or for most part in the hands of private individuals or other private enterprises so that the state cannot directly influence them; and finally, that this private sphere of economic activity can be seen to influence the macro-economic behaviour of the whole system, the trend of changes in the level of employment, income, prices and wages and the cyclical fluctuations round this trend. By state ownership of the means of production we mean that, apart from certain exceptions which are insignificant from the standpoint of the economy as a whole, every economic organisation is subordinate to a unified state administrative hierarchy, and the allocation of productive resources is arranged among the different levels and branches of this hierarchy. Neither income, nor decision-making rights stem from any sort of capital market. (It goes without saying that state property as defined here is not the only possible form of non-capitalist property relation.)

Economic organisation

The models of a capitalist economy can be ranged on a scale

between two extremes. In the one ideal type a perfectly competitive market links the enterprises with the consumers, while in the other the enterprises are powerful corporations which can cut themselves off completely from market conditions. In the former model, as far as the enterprise is concerned, the market parameters are an objective datum which has to be adapted to. In the latter model the enterprises do not adapt themselves to the economic environment, but rather mould the economic environment to suit their own investment, development and production programmes.

It is clear that the latter ideal type is closer to the model of the Soviet economy than the "pure competition" ideal type. It is also a commonplace to say that historical development by now is in the process of passing from the situation of the first ideal type to that of the second. At most, what is disputed is the degree of concentration and centralisation that has been reached. Both standpoints incline us to assume for the purposes of the present study that independence from market forces has proceeded as far as is possible under capitalism. Thus we ought only to set out those limitations to development which can in no way be transgressed while private ownership of the means of production is dominant.

Under capitalism the joint effect of two things hinders the elimination of the mechanisms of supply and demand. One of these is the uncertainty of the conditions of economic activity. No growth and integration of corporations is entirely indifferent to unforeseeable changes in the economic environment. There are always incalculable changes in the sphere of the supply of raw materials, in technological development and in the structure of the labour supply. That is, even the biggest corporations cannot completely control the input of production factors. Neither can consumer demand be perfectly manipulated. Manipulation is merely one of the factors that affect consumer preferences, and no one can say for certain how manipulation influences the structure of demand and its overall size. As a result, the possibilities for both investment and profits fluctuate, and do so, moreover, in a way which cannot be completely foreseen and is not always the same. It is not possible, therefore, to be entirely free from the uncertainties of the supply of and demand for capital.

The second thing which limits the changeover to programmed production is the institutional system of the capitalist economy. Complicated relationships of dependence are created between capitalist enterprises by the overlapping of shareholdings and board membership. One corporation buys a significant portion of the shares of another; a significant portion of the shares of two corporations are in the property of one person or family group; two enterprises have common members on their boards or in their executive management, etc. Similar links can exist between a private enterprise and the state as well. The state can buy shares in a private enterprise and, vice versa, private enterprises and private individuals can buy shares in state enterprises. But these relations of mutual dependence do not conquer the whole of the economy. Many big groups exist in the capitalist economy which really are independent of each other and of the state. It follows from this that capitalist enterprises are typically self-financing, that is, they must cover their expenditure by their income. Thus they cannot shift the risk costs on to other economic organisations, but must accommodate themselves to the unforseeable changes of environment, that is to market conditions.

The only economic organisation for which this condition does not hold true in the strict sense is the state. The majority of the state's income does not come from productive, service or commercial activities, and usually the use of income is not determined by the aim of creating new income from it. State budgeting can therefore play the role of a shock-absorber when, for example, a mammoth enterprise is on the verge of bankruptcy. In the interests of ensuring employment and averting negative market reaction (or simply as a result of lobby pressure) the state can give the enterprise temporary tax concessions or can even aid it with exceptional credits and advantageous orders. What is more, the state can act relatively freely when it decides on this kind of intervention, for not only is it able to use the financial and physical resources at its disposal to cover its costs, but it can, for example, also impose an exceptional tax or increase the money supply at a rate faster than that of economic growth, etc. On top of this, it can aid the economy by such methods as a statutory wages policy or by the use of statutory price regulation. But the freedom of the capitalist state is severely limited. It cannot raise taxes as it likes, since this decreases what is usually called the desire to invest. It cannot permanently keep the money supply above the level of growth, because this would lead to uncontrollable inflation and the destruction of the economic mechanism. Statutory wage and price regulations always leads to dubious results, unless control is extended to every sort of economic transaction, and the capitalist state is only capable of doing this in a war economy. In short, the capitalist state can only intervene in economic processes to the extent that it is allowed to by the behavioural patterns of the private economy. The private economy reacts to state intervention according to its own rules. If the state does not bring its actions into line with these patterns, then these actions become counter-productive; for example, anti-cyclical measures which are overdone or badly timed can have a destabilising effect.

The possibilities of independence from the economic environment are not unlimited in the Soviet-type system either, but they are nevertheless substantially greater. Here too it is impossible to foresee exactly the changes going on among production factors and consumer preferences. The principle of self-financing is valid too, at least in the context of the economy as a whole, for, to be sure, it is a tautology that in any closed system total expenditure cannot be bigger than total income plus total accumulated savings. But at the level of the individual enterprise it is not necessary to put this into effect. With the exception of significant small-scale industrial and commercial services, the whole economy is organised under a single, unitary administrative hierarchy. As with the capitalist economy, this also has two ideal types, and here too development is from one towards the other. The first is the centralised ideal type. Here the central powers prescribe in detail what to produce, in what quantities, to what standard, using what quality of tools and what materials, and in accordance with these orders, with a separate planning order on each occasion, they put the necessary resources at the enterprises' disposal. In this case the enterprises are, by definition, not self-financing, for they do not operate with resources which are permanently at their disposal. They are not financially responsible for their losses. The accumulation of unsold goods is not for them an indication of the need to change the structure of production. The second is the decentralised ideal type. Here the central powers set only very general targets for the enterprises (for example, they must achieve a given profit) and the enterprises dispose of their own resources, with which they fulfil their targets. In this case the enterprises can be self-financing, but the economy can also function normally if, de facto, no single enterprise is self-financing (which naturally is not the same as saying that total growth is negative, for the surpluses taken by the state can be greater than the losses incurred by the enterprises).

The decentralisation of the command system does not mean that the enterprises gain institutional autonomy from the state. Dependence remains, even if it is not accompanied by the right of command over every detail of enterprise activity. Enterprise directors are appointed and dismissed, rewarded and punished, by the central powers: that is, by just those same units of the hierarchical organisation which, by the manipulation of the state budget and bank credits, control the investment possibilities of the enterprises, while on the other hand also controlling, via the party and the trade unions, the consensus between the interest groups within the enterprise.

Let us consider the example of investments. Suppose that the investment system is ideally decentralised: that is to say, discounting all infrastructural and non-economic investments, that every investment decision originates at enterprise level. From this it does not yet follow that every investment will be covered from its own savings. Just like the capitalist corporation, the Soviet-type enterprise is dependent on external investment sources. But while the search for external investment sources renders the capitalist enterprise dependent on the capital and money markets where the state and private capital compete with one another, the Soviet-type enterprise becomes dependent on the state administrative hierarchy. A Soviet-type enterprise can, in principle, draw on three sources: another enterprise's capital, bank credits and support from the state budget. The first possibility in reality is insignificant, even in the extreme case of there being no legal barriers to it. It is not in the interests of the individual departments directing the economy to agree to allow outside enterprises, which they cannot directly control, to gain influence over enterprises under their supervision by investing capital in them. Nor is it in the interests of the enterprises to invest their capital in an area where the power of a distant branch of the administrative hierarchy holds sway. As far as the other two sources are concerned, the central powers exercise exclusive control over them. The enterprises can compete with one another for budget support or bank credits, but the central apparatus does not compete with anyone for investment demand. Real investment decisions, in consequence, generally originate with the participation of the central authorities, even if the investment system is ideally decentralised.

There is no legal autonomy of enterprises to limit the Soviet-type state's direct influence on enterprise behaviour. This influence is not even restricted by the fact that obedient enterprises are recompensed for relative or absolute losses incurred by state intervention. In the first place, it has at its disposal a larger arsenal of instruments with which to balance enterprise finances. On top of the measures that the capitalist state can use (tax concessions, credit supports) the Soviet-type state can take further specific measures because it controls the interest to be paid on productive capital, determines the wage fund to be used by the enterprise and its mode of distribution, and also regulates the price system. Secondly, the Soviet-type state can use these tools more freely than the capitalist one can use its tools. The only things which limit its actions are those such as the *de facto* macroeconomic ratios of the budget (for example, it cannot curtail for a long period the portion allocated to ensure a socially acceptable level of consumption), but it is not restricted by the anticipations and unpredictable reactions of enterprises. To stay with the example of investments, the state does not have to be afraid of the desire to invest falling because of frequent disturbances in the price system or the redistribution of the whole of the surplus to loss-making enterprises. First of all, the overwhelming majority of investments are conceived with the participation of the state, so the state can thus influence them directly. Secondly, the enterprises are not deterred by unsatisfactory demand, as they can count on state support in the case of making a loss.

Both economies, capitalist and Soviet, are mixed economies. In both, some mixture of market and non-market relations co-ordinates the processes of production, service and consumption. However, the private property barrier in capitalism does not allow non-market relations to come to gain precedence. However much the freedom of the state and the large corporations is increased, the market always remains the primary frame of reference to which non-market actions must adapt themselves. State property (as defined above) is not a barrier to non-market actions. Rather, the hierarchical relations of dependence between the central command and the enterprises put restrictions on the market becoming the dominant frame of reference. And if this difference holds even in this imaginary marginal case, where the two systems are closest to each other, then *a fortiori* it must stand in all other cases, that is, in the comparison between really existing capitalist and really existing Soviet societies.

The class structure

At first glance the difference seems to be that each class, including the working class, has its own economic and political organisations under capitalism, while in Soviet-type societies no class, not even the ruling class, is capable of organising itself independently. But there would be no point in incorporating this difference in the explanatory model. The part of this statement referring to capitalist societies, though valid for most developed Western nations, is true only with important exceptions: fascism and military dictatorships. Rather, we should go back to very general differences to find the reason why it is so common, under capitalism, for independent class organisations to be incorporated into the reproduction process of society, and why, in Soviet-type societies, it never occurs.

If we set aside the problems of the organisation of classes, a single essential structural difference remains, namely the differences in the ruling class's relation to property. In brief, under capitalism the ruling class has a property-owning stratum, in Soviet-type societies, on the other hand, it does not.

Those marxists who say that the two systems work in an essentially similar way do not attribute any significance to this difference. They either argue that in modern capitalism real economic power does not lie in the hands of the property-owning group, or they argue that the ruling class of Soviet-type societies is a property-owning class as well, that it is in command of the forces of production of the whole society in the same way as the shareholders of a large corporation are in command of the corporation's capital. Let us consider the former contention first. It is based on the well-known thesis of academic sociology and economics on the separation of ownership and control. The bigger the corporations, the more fragmented the ownership of capital and the smaller the proportion of shares that remain in private hands. As a result, the growth of corporations inevitably reaches a point where the shareholders cannot already influence the economic strategy of the enterprise with their votes. From that point onwards it is not the corps of owners that makes real economic decisions, but the summit of the enterprises' organisational hierarchy, the upper management. Private property becomes a mere epiphenomenon; it has its effects on the field of the distribution of income and differences of consumption, but it has no influence on economic and political power. Real power, just as in Soviet-type societies, is linked to key positions in the large organisations, the corporations and the state.

In accordance with our method of reasoning, we shall accept that this thesis of the separation of ownership and control is in fact valid, even though we realise that the empirical evidence to back up the thesis is extremely controversial and that precisely among sociologists the opposite thesis has much support. But if, even in this marginal case, we find significant differences in the structure of the capitalist and socialist ruling class, then we do not have to prove separately that the difference holds when we look at other individual cases.

Now let us suppose that shareholders cannot in fact influence positively the behaviour of management with their votes. They can still, however, influence it in a negative way. If they are dissatisfied with their dividend, they can withdraw their capital from the company. Therefore, as long as capital is freely alienable, that is to say, as long as the capital market exists, the managers of large corporations will be forced to behave, by and large, exactly as the owner-directors of the traditional profit-maximising enterprises. The economic power of management is indeed linked to organisational roles and not to legal property rights, but behind the organisations stand separate property interests. In the case of the complete separation of ownership and control, these interests control decision-making by means of an anonymous power only: the power of the capital market. But this power is enough to keep the corporations in their sphere of influence. Therefore, management cannot simply merge with the state technocracy; it cannot become the representative, at company level, of interests linked to the state apparatus. Under capitalism, a not insignificant portion of the ruling class is made up of private individuals, who as a social group, supported by independent economic power, manoeuvre against the other classes and groups within the ruling class.

The other proposition remains, according to which the ruling class of Soviet-type societies is nothing more than a kind of "collective property" class. And indeed, all the power that under capitalism is attached to private enterprises, in these societies is divided between the various levels and branches of the administrative hierarchy. However, we should not forget that in Soviet-type economic systems there are no functional equivalents to such institutions as general meetings of shareholders or the capital market. There are no specialised organisations which might call the efficiency of the utilisation of invested capital to account, and which can freely transfer their capital from one enterprise to the other if they are dissatisfied with the results. Ownership functions are distributed between the various parts of the administrative apparatus and are, at the same time, impossibly intertwined with their non-ownership functions: for example, the tasks of ensuring political stability and macro-economic balances. In Soviet-type societies a person belongs to the ruling class inasmuch as, and only inasmuch as, he plays a role in making and/or preparing decisions within the state administrative hierarchy. All his power is tied to his office or to informal relationships which have been established during his official activities. His power has no private backing separate from the state administrative hierarchy. Therefore it is misleading to call the ruling class a "collective property" class.

In Soviet-type societies, all sections of the ruling class are clearly subordinate to the top political élite, which monopolises the summits of the state administrative hierarchy. Decentralisation of the command system does, of course, increase the freedom of decision of the lower branches, but it does not create independent economic powers which would cut across the relations of sub- and superordination of the administrative apparatus. Even the enterprise managements in an ideally decentralised system do not stand at the head of autonomous economic organisations. They are not controlled by the capital market, and not even by some sort of functional equivalent of it, but by the uniform administrative hierarchy, and in the last analysis by the political élite of the ruling class. And if we find that the chances of class organisation and the possible forms of class struggle are substantially different even in this marginal case, in which the two class structures are closest to each other, then the difference must stand *a fortiori* in all other cases as well.

The consequences

Let us first take the examples that the Western marxist left cite when they say that there is no substantial difference between the two systems: the hierarchical division of labour, technological development and the structure of consumption. Then we shall discuss a phenomenon which sharply refutes the convergence theory: the dynamic of economic cycles. Finally we shall examine the question that is at the centre of every marxist enquiry: what are the possibilities in both systems for organised class struggle?

The convergence thesis is correct in pointing to the fact that the social organisation of the economic units of production, factories and enterprises, reveals a conspicuous similarity in both capitalist and Soviet-type societies. In both systems, the positions determined by the formal organisation of economic units can be articulated into a hierarchy according to the extent to which their occupants dispose of the material factors of production, and the extent to which they have power over the individuals taking part in production. In both societies this hierarchy runs parallel with the ladder of income and prestige. And in both societies, exactly the same ideology of inevitable technological necessity justifies these social inequalities. Modern technology, it is claimed, requires that the direct producers should be mere executors of primary work tasks. On the other hand, the planning and co-ordination of these primary work tasks requires mental labour based on a high level of qualification, that must be rewarded by society with the appropriate privileges.

In both societies the more or less unified ladders of power, prestige and income extend beyond the boundaries of the primary economic units of production as well. But the models sketched above draw attention to an important difference. Under capitalism, this extension of the production and company hierarchy does not correspond to a hierarchy of organisational roles on the model of a formal organisation. In Soviet-type societies, however, the hierarchy of factories and enterprises is part of the unified state administrative hierarchy. Under capitalism, the highest level of the hierarchy of society can be seen only as a social stratum. It is not homogeneous in an organisational sense. The people at the top of the independent economic, political, state administrative, scientific organisations, etc., all belong to this stratum; furthermore, there are the people who, irrespective of which organisation they belong to, have got into the social élite by way of inherited material and cultural privileges. In Soviet-type societies, on the other hand, the hierarchy of the unified state administrative organisation itself defines the social élite.

This distinction is based on the structure of the formal organisations and the relations between them. Thus the question is posed as to whether the difference itself is not also formal.

It could be argued that under capitalism the formally independent organisations are in reality interdependent, that those economic and cultural privileges which do not depend on the organisations are losing their traditional significance. If, however, we accept the (immediately plausible) condition of our model that under capitalism at least a significant part of the economic organisations are not only independent but directly competitive with each other, then we can realise the significance of this situation. Each section of the capitalist ruling class must set up separate organisations alongside or above the competitive economic organisations, if it wants to synchronise the behaviour of its members to an extent which informal coalitions are incapable of ensuring. For the Soviet ruling class, however, the creation of such organisations would mean the very undoing of the institutionally given unity of the ruling class.

Another possible objection is that the hierarchy of the division of labour within the factory is exactly the same, whether it is a part of a unified administrative hierarchy or not. Has the difference which our model indicates got any relevance to the situation of the direct producer, the over-specialised, repetitive nature of work, the technical separation of the spheres of decision-making and execution? Now this objection must be accepted in so far as it concerns the working class, or at least the working class in the traditional sense. But it does not follow that it is valid for every social group whose members take part in the production of material goods and services and who, like the traditional working class, have no power over the others involved in production. There is a substantial difference, in the two societies, between the nature of productive activity for which communication transcending the institutional and enterprise barriers is necessary. The tensions caused by the hierarchical organisation of scientific and culturally creative activity pass as commonplaces in Western critical sociology, given that the precondition for the optimal development of such creative activity is non-authoritarian communication. On the basis of our model, it is not difficult to see that in Soviet-type societies these tensions are manifest in a different and much stronger manner.

For simplicity's sake, let us confine ourselves to scientific research work. The function of the hierarchical organisation of research under capitalism is not to replace the channels of non-authoritarian communication through which the consensus of the scientific community emerges. The openly avowed function of hierarchical structure in this case is to intensify communication in those areas which are especially important from the standpoint of the organisation's own economic, military, political ends, etc., or to put the results achieved in these areas into a directly usable form. Naturally, this influence introduces authoritarian elements into the communication of the scientific community and restricts its autonomy. But however great this influence is, the situation of the scientific community is substantially different under capitalism from what it is in Soviet-type societies. In the latter, the hierarchical organisation of scientific research is not only required for the utilisation of research results. As the internal hierarchy of the research organisations is an extension of the hierarchy of the appropriate branch of the unitary state administrative organisation, the conflicts between the hierarchical organisation of research and the autonomy of the scientific community in Soviet-type societies always have a political undertone. The administrative apparatus cannot tolerate the emergence of free non-authoritarian communication channels within any social group which might form the basis of independent self-organisation, for such tendencies endanger its informational and organisational monopoly. Thus it cannot allow scientists to go beyond the bounds of personal contact and give public expression to their dissenting opinions on the preferences for certain research programmes, the social use of science and the institutional framework of research. What is more, it also tries to limit as far as possible the forms of personal communication in which dissenting opinions of this type can circulate. It does everything to prevent the emergence of scientific schools or trends which cut accross the organisational forms of the formal hierarchy, and tries to keep the communications between researchers under control. Of course, the complete elimination of autonomy would lead science to atrophy and would be accompanied by intolerable economic and military disadvantages. A certain degree of freedom of communication and opinion-forming is therefore experienced by scientific researchers even under the strictest political control, and this puts them, together with the producers of culture, in a privileged position by comparison with other social groups, at least as far as the attainable level of ideological self-consciousness and coherence is concerned. But concessions of this sort never go as far as creating those conditions for non-authoritarian communication within the scientific community which, under capitalism, still count as the normal conditions of research.

In some contemporary Soviet-type societies the contradictory requirements of the maintenance of hierarchical organisation and the ensuring of non-authoritarian communication are being balanced out in the form of a compromise. Even in social science, it is exceptional for the apparatus to dictate the solution of questions of content. It is more a question of taboos on certain enquiries. But the academic community can only ensure this degree of real autonomy for itself if it not only completely surrenders its right to participate in decisions on organisational problems or financing research, but again and again ritually endorses the right of the apparatus to influence the content of research results from an ideological and political point of view. In return, the apparatus does not exercise this right continually, but usually leaves it to the scientific community itself to exercise ideological control and unofficial censorship over its "deviant" members. At all events, this puts the brakes on scientific development. And the continuing existence of the compromise has the result of barring from the research organisations a section of the new generation of intellectuals who are unable to master or unwilling to accept the rules of the game.

If, as we did in another chapter, we were to widen the circle of the initial conditions of our model, and if we were to use it to study the situation of the Soviet intelligentsia, we would be able to show that this marginalised intelligentsia finds its living at a lower level, in auxiliary jobs in the sphere of organised research. It is capable of more or less retaining its intellectual lifestyle and the habits of communication that go with it, but it lies clearly outside the official intelligentsia. In every East European country this sub-intellectual group creates the social basis for a counter-culture. And on this base, as the example of the Soviet Union shows, even clandestine religious, cultural and political movements can also evolve.

Technological development

At first glance we might think that the difference between the models in this area is of no consequence. The transformation to a humanised technostructure which would allow the hierarchical division of labour to be dismantled is not in the interests of either ruling class, and in neither society is the oppressed class capable of enforcing such technological alternatives. It appears that the differences stem only from the differing point of departure, i.e. the relative backwardness of East European societies, and that in any case the differences are continually decreasing. But if we think through the consequences of our model more deeply, then it comes clear that the technological backwardness of Soviet-type societies originates in the working of the system itself, that it constantly reproduces itself, though always at a higher level; thus the imitation of proven Western technology, irrespective of the interests of the ruling class or of working-class pressure, is so advantageous economically that it makes any alternative *ab ovo* illusory. Thus the trend of technological development in the two societies is not similar because the same trend stems from the nature of both societies. It is similar because there is an inbuilt technological backwardness in the Soviet-type economic model, and this makes it more likely that the Soviet economy will choose the path of borrowing ready-made solutions.

Let us compare the effect of the workings of the two types of economic organisation on technological development. Capitalist economic organisations are motivated essentially by three desires when they experiment with and introduce technical innovation. These are interlinked but easily separable at this abstract level of analysis: to economise on production factors, to stimulate demand, and to gain an advantage in the exploitation of as yet vaguely outlined technical possibilities, since this advantage may be of decisive importance in competing with other organisations, once the economic significance of the new technology has become clear. If we examine how these desires manifest themselves in the Soviet-type economy, we shall find that all three are achieved much less vigorously than under capitalism.

The saving on production factors is a constant desire of the Soviet economic administration too. Decentralisation and the growth of purely economic indicators of success have made it possible for this desire to a certain extent to influence enterprise decisions. But as a result of the peculiar characteristics of the system, it is still not always in the interest of the enterprise to run the risks that accompany the experimentation with, and introduction of, technological innovations. It is often advantageous for the enterprise, in bargaining with the higher organs of economic administration, to refer to its level of technical equipment as a sort of unchangeable datum, and to try to get more resources on the basis of the fact that it is forced to use up a larger than normal amount of certain production factors.

The stimulation of demand plays an insignificant role in the technical development strategy of a Soviet-type economy. The situation of its consumer goods market is directly determined by the backwardness of the starting conditions. Under the influence of information flooding from the mass media, the consumers go for those goods which dominate the consumer market of developed capitalist nations. On the producer goods market, on the other hand, it clearly follows from our model that even in the most decentralised system the play of supply and demand is very small.

There remains the third desire. In Soviet-type societies this is naturally present only in the highest circles of economic management, which in itself does not amount to a disadvantage. Results in this field depend on the size of expenditure, the discovery of promising new areas of possibilities and an adequate level of scientific research. However, it is at this very point that new scientific results dictate their influence on technical development, because the size of investment means that the detailed control of scientific research is at its strictest. The continuing retardation of scientific research which we mentioned under the first point entails clearly distinguishable economic disadvantages.

The structure of consumption

Earlier we ventured the statement that the Soviet-type economy is imitating the supply structure that has developed in the consumer market of the developed capitalist countries. This appears directly to contradict the initial proposition of our model. Does it not follow from our model that the Soviet-type economy has more difficulty accommodating itself to the evolution of individual consumer demand? Is it not cheaper to develop collective services in a centrally administered economy than to satisfy the demand for consumer durables used in individual households? Does not the ruling élite of Soviet-type societies have all the instruments necessary to turn the development of consumption towards communal services? To the first two questions we must reply with an ambiguous "yes". The final question, however, requires more detailed discussion.

In principle, the unitary system of economic management might make it possible to establish the domination of communal services. The central powers, in principle, have the tools to slow down the rise in money incomes, to regulate more forcefully the market of consumer goods in a way that is more in tune with the balancing ability of the centralised economy so that an ever-growing ratio of communal services are made to operate in the direct distribution system. The worker and employee strata are unable to control central decisions of this kind; at most they can express their dissatisfaction in the form of amorphous pressure. But in a paradoxical way, the uncontrollable nature of the power of the ruling class in this field restricts its room for manoeuvre. Because of their very inability to exercise control over the distribution of communal services, the worker and employee strata strive chiefly to increase their money incomes. They try to solve their consumption problems in ways that nobody has a say over. The system can only withstand this desire by using the weapon of mass terror. If the stability of the system does not rest solely on open violence, but rather, among other things, on some sort of consensus among the population, then it cannot but allow these pressures. And once the rise in the production of individual consumer goods and money incomes has started, then with time the process becomes self-sustaining. More and more investment ties both the households and the producing and marketing enterprises to the organisation of consumption on the Western model. This provides a foundation and infrastructure for the consumer goods industry and trade, on the basis of which it is always more economical to satisfy the various individual demands along the Western model than to embark on a communal service development programme, which incurs heavy initial capital costs and a very slow return on this capital, though eventually it would lead to cheaper services, at least in principle. The retention of the existing structure conforms better to the monetary equilibrium of the economic system than changing it. If the production of individual consumer goods decreased and the expenditure on communal services increased proportionately, there would be tension on the consumer goods market between the commodity supply and the population's money income. On the other hand, in the area of communal services, investment demand would exceed the available resources.

In the 1960s, in almost every Soviet-type society, this development became irreversible, though not to the same extent everywhere. The reduction of systematic mass terror in the second half of the 1950s made it necessary to raise significantly the level of consumption in a relatively short space of time. Money incomes had to be raised suddenly, and the consumer goods market had to be quickly filled to a corresponding degree. In such circumstances there were no resources left for the long term development of communal services. The process began with an increase in the supply of everyday consumer goods and gradually spread to consumer durables. In some East European countries a significant part of the housing supply is even administered via market forms. In every East European country they have produced in sufficent numbers the necessary appliances for the development of self-contained family household service units, and everywhere the consumer complex of the motor car is growing quickly.

The growing predominance of private consumption clearly brings with it all those phenomena at which left-wing social criticism is directed in the West: the scramble for material goods at the household level, the wasteful use of resources, and the upsetting of the ecological balance at the level of society as a whole. But if we bear in mind that this analagous pattern of consumption is produced by different mechanisms in Soviet-type societies, then we must also recognise that the social effect of the process is not exactly the same here as under capitalism. Here, the growth in the role of private consumption has a consequence which is positive beyond all doubt. It increases the economic independence of the population in relation to the centrally administered economic organisations. In the long run we must consider this a very important development, even if we are unable to foresee its exact consequences. It is not impossible that it will be accompanied by a strengthening of personal nonconformism within the working class, especially among the younger generation, for whom the greater economic security of the parental household means, temporarily, a greater freedom of movement and a lesser obligation to earn money.

Economic cycles

Economic growth in both systems is cyclical by nature, that is, it does not move forward along a balanced trajectory, whose parameters it might keep to indefinitely, but rather fluctuates more or less violently around a general course. The behaviour of the two systems is also similar inasmuch as, in both, investment cycles determine other fluctuations. The investment cycles themselves, however, differ substantially in numerous fundamental characteristics between the two systems. For the moment we shall confine ourselves to the differences observable at the upper and lower points of the cycle, and try to relate them to the model of the two systems.

Under capitalism, the investment boom does not generally go to the limits of physical capacity which would render impossible an unchanged growth rate in all current investments. By limits of physical capacity, we mean that the quantity of raw materials flowing into production cannot be increased correspondingly with demand, that the growth in the amount of construction equipment has not been quick enough to put into production, in an acceptable period of time, all the investment that has begun, and that the reserves in the labour force have been completely used up, etc. Nor is it usual under capitalism for a material shortage in commodity supply to set limits on an unchanged rate of growth of investment. This latter phenomenon occurs when investments rise so quickly over a relatively long period of time that, because of the imbalance in the distribution of the national income, the production of consumer goods cannot keep pace with the flow of income resulting from increased employment. The economic brakes of the capitalist enterprise come into operation before the investment boom has bumped into these obstacles, and they then reverse the whole process.

In Soviet-type economic systems, on the other hand, the upper point of the cycle is usually only reached when resources have become physically inadequate for the maintenance of the rate of investment, or when the physical inadequacies of commodity supply necessitate a transfer of resources. In smaller countries, which are extremely sensitive to foreign trade and where there is a way of temporarily mitigating the lack of resources or consumer goods by way of an increase in imports and restrictions on exports, the absolute upper point of the investment boom is linked to the deficit in the foreign trade balance. But in all cases the change is brought about by serious supply difficulties and production jams: the kinds of operational disorder which under capitalism usually occur as the result of the turn of the cycle, and even then usually only in those rare cases when an exceptionally severe crisis, not an ordinary recession, follows an exceptionally speculative boom. This means that we get a one-sided picture of the development of mass consumption in Soviet-type societies if we only pay attention to the general trend. The level of mass consumption is rising slowly but surely, only this ascending movement is periodically broken by more or less severe problems of supply which can be accompanied by attempts to squeeze the real income of the working class. The high point of the investment cycle therefore often coincides with an increase in the dissatisfaction of the population. In especially serious cases the upper limit can coincide wth classic bread riots or similar upheavals.

On the other hand, only seldom does the overrunning of the boom have to be paid for by a protracted recession or depression. The holding back of investment lasts only until physical capacities, or the flow of consumer goods, are increased enough (or foreign trade is balanced enough) for the upward process to start again. The crisis is never one of overproduction, it is always the crisis of a shortage economy.

When we set up our model of the two economic systems, we noted that the desire of the capitalist entrepreneur to invest changes as a function of the expected return on capital (more precisely: of the expected profit flow from investment, of the costs of investment and of the general rate of interest), while in Soviet-type economies the efficiency of investment in no way influences the enterprise's insatiable hunger for that investment. This difference explains the variations in behaviour of the two systems around the upper and lower turning-points of the cycle.

Under capitalism, as the investment boom begins to exhaust capacities and to increase significantly the number of investments competing with each other, investment costs increase, expected income decreases, and at the same time, as a result of the increased demand for money, the rate of interest rises. These changes can take place either relatively smoothly or with dramatic suddenness, according to the part played by the investors' "unjustified optimism" in the period before the upturn. But there have to be especially strong temptations to speculate if the enterprises are not to react at all to the rise in the price of increasingly scarce resources until the very moment when the increase in investments actually reaches the limits of physical capacity or the physical limits of consumer commodity supply. In normal circumstances, the willingness to invest begins to decrease much earlier and brings with it a decline in the growth of all production. And similarly, it is not enough for the capitalist economy to get out of a recession or depression for a rise in the rate of investment to become physically possible. Before this, all the changes which make the capitalist entrepreneur's expectations favourable have to take place: the decrease in unsold stock, the re-establishment of "confidence", etc.

In Soviet-type economies there are no built-in brakes of this sort, neither to the boom nor to the new upturn. Enterprises are insensitive to losses accompanying an increase in investments, and therefore exert a continual pressure on the central authorities in favour of increasing the investment funds. On the other hand, the central authorities are incapable of withstanding this pressure. For one thing, investment support is one of the tools by which they reward those enterprises which toe the line. They are obliged to use it in their bartering with enterprise management. For another thing, the central authorities are generally unable to forecast the real cost of individual investments. The applicant almost always has ways of obtaining the approval of the state planning and financial departments on the basis of unrealistically low cost calculation, and once the investment has started, the central authorities will allow the extra expenditure necessary for completion sooner or later in any case. In Soviet-type economies, therefore, the forces urging over-investment control the distribution of the national income, even when the central plan does not set the maximum possible growth-rate of investments as a target. In reality, however, the parallel effect of these two desires, the investment hunger of the enterprises and the ambition of the central authorities, almost always jointly determines the dynamics of the economic cycle.

On the other hand, once the investment halt called for by the disruption of the balance has had its effect, and once the acceleration of investment has become physically possible again, then there is no economic barrier to the upswing. As soon as the strictures on new investments and on the offering of investment supports or credits are relaxed, the scramble for investment resources begins again.

Class struggle

We have already touched on the basic difference in the political institutional system of the two societies, in our outline of the models. In the majority of capitalist societies, every social group has the means of representing its own interests in relation to decisions of state power via its own political organisations, while in Soviet-type societies not even the ruling class has such organisations. Now, in conclusion, we must relate these characteristics in the behaviour of the two systems to the explanatory model.

The economic activity of the bourgeoisie takes place in the private sector of society. This economic activity naturally always influences the decisions of the state authority, and this influence, as we suggested when we sketched out our model, is becoming stronger. But we also suggested that the private nature of the workings of capitalist economic organisations does not change, which also means that within the bourgeoisie there are groups which stand in a competitive relation to one another. Each one would like to secure for itself the advantages of co-operation with the state, would like the infrastructural investments of the state to be decided in its favour, would like itself to be the one to receive advantageous state orders, etc. But they are not all equally strong in their competitive struggle to influence the state's economic policy. And the weaker groups would be forced to look on helplessly as the links of the stronger lobby with the state became closed and more exclusive, if they could not resort to other mechanisms for influencing the decisions of the state authority which might make it possible for them to balance their economic disadvantages with certain non-economic advantages. These mechanisms are guaranteed to the opposing groups of the bourgeoisie by the system of so-called representative democracy. The ratios of representation are defined by the exercise of political rights attached to the individual; the competing groups of the bourgeoisie thus have the opportunity not merely to measure their own strength against that of the others, but also to try and gather behind themselves the forces of the other classes in society. And because of the very inequality of the positions of economic power, there are always, within the bourgeoisie, not insignificant groups who have an interest in maintaining the representative system as a mechanism for balancing the power relations within the ruling class.

Naturally, individuals invested with equal political rights in a system based on the exercise of political rights attached to the individual do not all influence the decisions of the state authority with equal weight. The strength of the political organisations and tools for influencing public opinion are determined to a great extent by the weight of the economic power behind them. To this extent, the ratios of the economic power of the various capitalist interest groups are realised even in the public sphere of political competition. But to some extent, economic strength in this field can be balanced by appeals to the interests of the electors.

What is more, the contest does not necessarily remain the internal affair of the competing groups of the bourgeoisie. Once institutions of political democracy exist, the other classes, including the working class, cannot be prevented from creating their own political organisations and tools for influencing public opinion. The political behaviour of the working class thus becomes less spontaneous and more predictable, and is enacted increasingly within a legal framework. The political content of the struggle within this framework decides what this means for the stability of the whole of the system. It can just as easily mean the growing integration of the aspirations of the working class as the intensification of the class struggle. But even in the latter case, the bourgeoisie cannot easily dismantle the institutional system of representative democracy, even if it is slowly becoming dangerous. The transformation of political institutions towards dictatorship affects the interests of the various groups among the bourgeoisie in different ways. Even within the capitalist class, therefore, factions evolve which adhere to the political institutional system that is advantageous for them, though by this they put the rule of the whole class at risk.

The political rights of the individual are by and large the same in Soviet-type societies as they are in liberal democracies. But no special group, not even the ruling class, has either the right or the means to influence the exercise of these rights through organisations and means of information which are centred solely on the interests of that group. So the exercise of political rights becomes an empty ritual. The formally existing representative institutions perform a symbolic function only. The ruling class does not need to enforce its influence on state power by way of any kind of political representation. Its rule is not based on its position in the private sector of the economy, but on its position in the state administrative hierarchy which abolishes the private nature of the economy. Naturally, the ruling class in Soviet-type societies is not unified either. Interest groups around the various levels and branches of the administrative hierarchy are continually struggling with each other for control over an increasingly large proportion of social resources. In normal circumstances, however, as far as we can see on the basis of our model at least, the structure of the system makes it disadvantageous for any group to break the unity of the administrative hierarchy.

If any group wanted to free itself from the administrative apparatus and tried to stand up as an independent economic power, it would not only find itself in opposition to the pressure of the other parts of the ruling class, but would also become defenceless against the oppressed class as well. The patronage of the political leaders does not only mean restrictions for the managers of productive and service enterprises, for example, but also defence against the workers. The upper economic administration guarantees that the "normal" demands of the workers can always be satisfied, and is able to mobilise sufficient force to break "excessive" demands. In normal circumstances the lower level managers desire, at most, the decentralisation of decision-making rights within the administrative hierarchy, and not the dismantling of the unity of the hierarchy.

As long as the unity of the administrative hierarchy remains, the oppressed class cannot create for itself an independent organisational base, for it always finds itself faced with the united pressure of the whole institutional system. The most important political consequences of our model, therefore, is that although the polarisation of the ruling class is a necessary precondition for an social force to organise itself, no developmental tendencies can be deduced from the general structure of the system which might point to the growth, with time, of the probability of such a polarisation.

For all that, the structure of the system does not exclude the appearance of crisis situations in which the unity of the ruling class is shaken. It was after such a crisis as this that the contemporary version of Soviet-type societies, the subject of our model, evolved. In the transition period immediately following the death of Stalin, that section of the ruling class which wanted to destroy the system of mass terror which threatened it too, tried, on occasions at least, to mobilise groups outside the ruling class against the old élite, which was directly involved in the exercise of terror. This was made possible by the fact that the ending of stalinist mass terror was in the primary interest of all the large social groups. The experiment, however, set off potentially revolutionary processes which threatened the very basis of ruling-class power and which in some countries could only be stopped by military means.

The political unity of the ruling class was re-established as a result of these shocks. No single interest group dared undertake so audacious an experiment. In the post-stalinist system that has taken root since the overcoming of the crisis, there is no ruling-class group at all whose interests might coincide with the aspirations of broader social strata. The contradictions are no longer so simple or clear-cut as they were at the time of the struggle for the ending of mass terror, when the whole "people" stood in opposition to a narrow political élite. Every social group is set on its own course now, determined by its partial interests. The target of the lower-level economic managers and political leaders, the chief forces in the destalinisation process, is to increase their economic power and their say in the preparation of upper-level decisions. For the masses the consequence is no longer manifest only in the ending of the mobilisation of everyday life, in the fact that basic consumer needs are relatively continuously satisfied, but in ever-increasing social differentiation, in ever-increasing contrasts of income, life-style and consumer habits. It is probable, therefore, that the behaviour of lower-level managers will gradually fit into the pattern that follows from our model; they will consciously orientate themselves towards decentralisation in the hierarchy, and cut themselves off from any attempt to break up the unity of the hierarchy.

It is not to be expected, therefore, that new crises in Soviet-type societies, that is, crises of the established post-stalinist system itself, will stem from shifts within the ruling class. Any new disruption of the ruling class can only conceivably take place, if at all, as the result of a crisis which has already exploded in reality. The crisis will thus either be the result of development tendencies which lead to the economic collapse of the system or to an increase in the capacity of the oppressed class to resist, or it will be the result of a change in external conditions which the system is no longer capable of adapting to. As far as the latter is concerned, the forecasting of such changes is not the task of abstract model building, but of concrete historical and sociological analysis. As far as the former two possibilities are concerned we have no reason, on the basis of our model, to predict that the collapse of the economic growth of Soviet-type societies must follow. We can make certain cautious predictions concerning the growth of the relative autonomy of the oppressed class (on the basis of the spread of intellectual nonconformism and the strengthened position of the workers' household), but we cannot deduce from our model alone that this tendency will transcend the limits of the system's tolerance. However, it does follow clearly from our model that once (for whatever reason) a political crisis evolves again, similar to the crisis of the transition period, it will be enacted at a higher level, among more differentiated forms. The ruling class has become more articulated as a result of decentralisation. Some of its groups have got used to greater independence. Ready oppositional ideologies have been developed in the subculture of the sub-intellectuals which, at the right moment, could have a mass effect. Illegal movements born in such an environment can have a certain importance in this sort of situation. The greater reserves of the workers' household give greater room for the emergence and consolidation of nonconformist ideas among groups of the younger generation now growing up in the working class.

Not sufficient? To be sure, it is not much. For post-stalinist development has only just begun, and there are scarcely any usable antecedents for a marxist theory of Soviet-type societies as *sui generis* class societies. Can people for whom the two systems are essentially the same say as much? Can they formulate in any way the problem of why there is no organised workers' movement, either revolutionary or reformist, in Eastern Europe? Can they explain why the members of the ruling class only realise their private interests by way of the role that they play in the administrative apparatus and not by way of independent political organisations? Can they account for the social basis of intellectual nonconformism? Do they recognise the possibilities latent in the rise of mass consumption? Can they explain the peculiar dynamic of economic cycles and their particular political effects? If not, the left-wing version of the convergence thesis must be discarded, and further progress must be made towards the elaboration of a theory of Soviet-type societies as *sui generis* class societies.

5 The Detours of East European Marxism

Soviet-type societies have so far never experienced the development of a marxism able to break away from official marxism on anything other than theoretical details, important or otherwise, and able to recognise that even its social basis cannot be the same as that of official marxism. The precondition for recognising that this social basis cannot be the same is that marxists should see Soviet-type societies as class societies in the strictest sense of the term, and should understand that it is simply a historical accident if the elements of the marxist tradition make up the ideology of the ruling class. Unofficial and even oppositional marxisms appear from time to time in Eastern Europe. There have been marxists who have sacrificed their freedom and even their lives for their beliefs. But no marxist has ever realised that the battle against the official ideology cannot aim, even in a secondary sense, at convincing and winning over the ruling class. Even those people who have criticised the policies of the apparatus in the name of the working class have in fact addressed themselves to the apparatus and not to the working class itself.

It seems that it could not have been otherwise: what marks the entire development of Soviet-type societies is the channelling of the proletariat's economic and political behaviour through institutions and organs over which the official ideology exercises a real monopoly. Anything which cannot be channelled in this way generally remains at the level of individual behaviour. And even when the accumulated energies are channelled neither through the official institutions nor through individual reactions but explode into spontaneous collective action, this remains an occasional and isolated event. These activities do not give rise to the autonomous forms of organisation which might enable an autonomous marxist theory to establish a mutual relationship with the practical formation of class consciousness.

It seems at first that marxism can find a social basis only within the apparatus. And in fact, the impression is that it is not simply the verbal marxism of the apparatus which has linked it with socialist traditions, but also the deeper commitment of at least a part of it. It has been precisely during those periods when it was possible to adopt independent ideological positions (in the 1920s in Russia and in the reform period of the late 1950s and 1960s in Eastern Europe) that the apparatus has been jolted by factional struggles. These struggles are evidently connected with the interests of the working class, even if it is in fact the interests of various groups of the ruling class which (somewhat less evidently) control them. One of the most important ideological signs of factional struggle is the intensified debate about marxism that takes place within the apparatus. Various tendencies appear, all claiming to offer the only true interpretation and application of the ideological tradition. In such conditions we should not be surprised at the paradoxical fact that there is a reversed relation between the search for a basis independent of the apparatus and the ideological debates within the apparatus. Breaking with the apparatus seems to mean renouncing the opportunity to exercise a practical influence on social processes. The only way of having some practical influence seems at first sight, in spite of all the compromises involved, to be to participate in the ideological debate inside the apparatus.

Marxism of the apparatus

The society which emerged from the earthquakes of revolution and civil war bore no resemblance to the social dream which had enticed the Bolshevik revolutionaries. It is true, though, that the former ruling classes had been annihilated on all sides; the nobility and the big landowners had disappeared once and for all from Russian history, and the bourgeoisie itself took such a blow that even the economic liberalism of NEP could not revive it. But the class enemy was not the only group to be destroyed: the very base of the Bolshevik party, the urban proletariat, was also annihilated. Only one force remained that was capable of action in urban Russia: the administrative apparatus, controlled by the party. This apparatus, whose organisational principles prevent social classes (including the new ruling class which forms around the apparatus) from facing the state as autonomous political forces, was not a result of the 1928-33 changes, it was the inheritance of the revolution itself.

But during the 1920s it had not yet extended its power to the whole of society. Revolution and civil war in the countryside had left behind them a society that was quite different. The peasantry emerged from the great changes as an autonomous economic power. It is true that after the land was redistributed the peasantry was mainly interested in its own internal affairs and its energy absorbed in parochial problems, and that the paralysis of the urban classes made it quite unlikely that it would regroup into forms of organisation extending beyond the village communities. But within the village boundaries the peasant was in charge. The party was unable to put down roots in the village, and the local organs of the central administration did not succeed in taking power from the village communities which had been revived by the revolutionary conflagration. The slightest jolt to the central power might have been enough to enable the peasantry to take advantage of its economic and social position and become an autonomous political force. The chronic economic tension between town and country made this political threat a concrete one. The democratisation of landed property automatically increased the agrarian population's consumption of its own products. This change in structure, together with the drop in agricultural production which followed the war and the complete disorganisation of industry, regularly threatened the urban population with famine.

The fate of the apparatus and the social order which it had established were dependent on its ability to overcome the economic and social heterogeneity of post-revolutionary Russia. It could neutralise the peasantry and guarantee at least a partial feeding of the urban population by temporarily using normal market channels of production for a time, during which it would be able to constitute an economic base for its superiority over the village; or it could extend its power to the villages by violence, and guarantee the degree of accumulation necessary for industrialisation by exploiting the peasantry to the maximum.

The historical leaders of the Bolshevik revolution were groping among these alternatives during the 1920s. But in their thinking, the aims of survival and holding on to power were constantly related to another aim: maintaining the proletarian nature of that power. They knew very well that society could fall apart if the ruling apparatus did not find a modus vivendi with the peasant commodity-producer. However, they treated the problem of survival not from the standpoint of the apparatus but from that of an (imaginary) working class. It was not the class power of the bureaucracy which they wished to shelter from the effects of freeing small-scale commodity production; it was socialism which they wished to shelter, both from the strengthening of small-scale commodity production and from the autonomy of the bureaucratic apparatus. While what they actually succeeded in doing was to probe the preconditions for a homogeneous hierarchy that would lead society, they were desperately trying to fight the consequences of this consolidation process.

While Lenin and Trotsky were aware of these antinomies, another variant of Bolshevism — theoretically and morally a more superficial one, but more important in the sociological sense — was taking shape: the Bolshevism of the apparatus. The apparatus never had any opportunity to ditch the Bolshevik traditions and create its own non-marxist ideology. Bolshevism had been institutionalised — in education, in the propaganda machinery and in the system for selecting officials. To oppose Bolshevism meant political disloyalty. But in any case, the apparatus had no interest in burying Bolshevik marxism. There were many things in Bolshevism that served the institutional and group interests of the established power-system very well. Above all — and in spite of all their attacks against the bureaucracy — Lenin and Trotsky themselves maintained the consensus that Soviet power was indeed the dictatorship of the proletariat and not that of some privileged social group. Besides, Bolshevism – by virtue of its marxist orthodoxy – was unequivocally committed to industrial development; because of this, it had defined the broad lines of development which the apparatus would in any case have to follow if it were to create the economic base for its political domination of the peasantry. And Bolshevism presented an image of the social stratification of the peasantry that indicated, at least roughly, what the government might expect from the village and how it could neutralise it.

But whatever the apparatus obtained from Bolshevism, the most important thing was neither the ideological justification for its power nor its general socio-economic orientation, but the principle of monolithic organisation. Because of the erosion of the urban classes and the fact that the peasantry had turned in on itself, the social discontent did not threaten to overthrow the directing apparatus from outside. The danger was rather that it would explode from within, either because of a split in the highest ranks of the leadership or because of the refusal of subordinate officials, who were in direct contact with the population, to execute unpopular decrees. And of course, by subordinating all individual differences of opinion to the organisational unity of the party, Bolshevism considerably reduced the danger that the ruling apparatus might fall apart, whether from above or from below. But on the other hand, it was Bolshevism itself that was one of the sources of dissenting activity, which had to be suppressed by merciless application of the Bolshevik disciplinary code. The workers' opposition, the trotskyist opposition, the united left opposition, the bukharinite opposition – groups were constantly forming within the party leadership that were at least partly inspired by the wish to carry out the theoretical principles of Bolshevism: to hand power back to directly democratic institutions, to replace dictatorship exercised in the name of the working class with the dictatorship of the working class itself, to re-establish freedom of expression and opinion in the party. These desires kept putting the interests of the ruling apparatus in danger, for even if they no longer had any large base outside the apparatus, they bore the threat of an organisational split within it. The apparatus needed a Bolshevism from which no such disagreeable consequences could be drawn. It need an ideology which would not claim to choose between just and unjust policies or "proletarian" and "non-proletarian" policies, but would give its blessing to any practical measures taken by those in power.

The history of marxism in Soviet Russia during the 1920s is chiefly a history of the process in which the apparatus adapted Bolshevik marxism to its own needs by crushing the successive oppositions. During this process, what we may call Soviet marxism – or better, stalinist ideology – was constituted. But the direction of this process only became clear with hindsight. The various theoretical positions which crystallised during the factional struggles appeared to most of the participants simply as different methods of applying Bolshevik marxism to the problems of the post-revolutionary situation. The tendency of the apparatus was to use detached parts of the theoretical tradition to further its own aims and to discredit its enemies politically, with total cynicism; but this was only gradually realised. And when it became clear that this was not a series of ad hoc manoeuvres but a coherent system, it was too late. Critical arguments were no use in the face of stalinist ideology, and Stalin's opponents had no access to the means of power after the end of the 1920s.

Leninism

In the beginning, the Bolsheviks simply wanted to be good disciples of the Second International's "orthodox marxists"; they wanted to apply marxism of the Kautsky-Plekhanov school as faithfully as possible to the particular situation of the Russian revolutionary workers' movement. And even later, after the political break with this school, they did not think of explaining their practical antagonisms in terms of theoretical divergences. They preferred to interpret them as the result of an individual about-turn on the part of their former teachers. And yet, while they thought they were applying the common theoretical tradition to a particular situation, they were moving away from "orthodox marxism" without noticing it.

The official marxism of the Second International contained something which was impossible to reconcile with any revolutionary workers' politics in backward Russia, and that was the proposition that there is an unambiguous causal relationship between the level of development of a country's productive forces and the maturity of the proletarian revolution. Even in the most developed capitalist countries it was easy to use this proposition to justify reformism, a passive waiting game, and the building up of the organisation for its own sake – even if none of these attitudes flowed logically from "orthodox marxism" (for the good reason that it had no clear criteria for determining the technical and economic level which put the revolution on the agenda). However, in the case of backward Russia the conclusion was unanimous: the proletariat could not become a revolutionary class there for a very long time yet.

The Bolsheviks tried to free themselves from this paralysing conclusion with the help of the idea of the revolution's international character. Capitalism, they said, is not an aggregate of closed national economies but a world system. As a result, the antagonisms which find a solution in the course of proletarian revolution are not those which occur between the forces and relations of production in a single country but those of the entire world capitalist system. It is highly unlikely that these antagonisms will break the chain of the world imperialist system in the more developed capitalist countries, for in these countries the internal contradictions are tempered by the advantages which the whole population draws from colonial exploitation and unequal exchange. The sparking point is rather to be found where the conflict between wage-labour and capital is sharpened by antagonisms which stem from the colonial or semi-colonial condition and from the difficulties of modernisation. It is true that the proletariat of these countries is weaker than the Western working class, but the bourgeoisie is even weaker and its socio-economic system even less viable. Such countries are heading inevitably for bourgeois democratic revolution – except that their bourgeoisies are incapable of leading it. The revolution must therefore be led by the proletariat, and since in this case the revolution cannot stop at the establishment of bourgeois democratic institutions, it has to go on to the dictatorship of the proletariat. This is the common content of Trotsky's theory of permanent revolution and Lenin's theory of imperialism.

But even if the Bolsheviks had a very unorthodox position on the dynamic of the revolution, they never thought of using this as a basis for revising the entire theory of "orthodox marxism". They pronounced that the centre of gravity of the world revolution had gone to the backward countries. But it never occurred to them that the backward countries could carry out autonomous revolutions on an autonomous social basis. For them, the only purpose of the Russian revolution was to give the signal for proletarian revolutions in the developed capitalist countries. If the European working class reacted to this signal, the Russian revolution could consolidate and make good its economic backwardness in a short space of time. If not, it would fail or degenerate. But whatever its fate, its task was in any case to create the kind of socio-economic structure which in the West was already in existence. The leading force of this revolution was the same: the proletariat. Of course, the Bolsheviks knew well that the peasantry's demographic and economic weight gave it a special place in the Russian revolution and in the transitional period which would follow the revolution. But they never thought of making the peasantry the leading class of the revolution, nor that the peasant economy and way of life could play any constructive role in the socialist society that had to be built.

It was the Bolsheviks' conception of the dynamic of the world revolution that enabled them to harmonise "orthodox marxism" with the aspirations of the Russian revolutionary workers' movement before 1917; and after 1917 it enabled them to harmonise "orthodox marxism" with the "irregular" features of Soviet power. They could carry out a proletarian revolution whose real measures were restricted to proclaiming peace, distributing the land and recognising the right of nationalities to self-determination. In order to strengthen the dictatorship of the proletariat, they allowed private production. They could be absolutely realist in their practice, just so long as they could tell themselves that with each new compromise they were prolonging the power of the soviets until dictatorships of the proletariat were proclaimed in Europe: in the favourable international situation that would thus ensue, they could undo all the compromises they had made. It was the wait for the world revolution that freed the Bolsheviks from looking the reality of the post-revolutionary class institutions and structures in the eye.

Lenin's thinking remained entirely within this circle of practical realism and theoretical orthodoxy. He expressed himself frankly when he was describing the measures taken by the Soviet government, and he was absolutely clear in his own mind as to the risk which these measures involved. But the risk for him was that the régime would fall and that capitalism would be restored. The idea that the power of the ruling apparatus could consolidate on a basis for which there was no formula in the theoretical tradition of Bolshevism simply did not occur to him. When NEP was instituted, he said outright that this amounted to a restoration of capitalism. But when he made such statements, he never thought that the development of Russian society could deviate from the route opened out by the proletarian revolution. We can recognise in all calmness that by freeing the market we are restoring capitalism, argued Lenin, because it is we who are freeing it. A capitalism which functions under the control of a proletarian state is not the same as the capitalism which functions in the capitalist countries. Soviet power finds itself forced to entrust the renewal of normal processes of production and distribution to the economic forces of capitalism, but at the same time as capitalism builds its own defensive positions, it prevents Soviet power from collapsing. It is hardly surprising that although Lenin often called this the restoration of capitalism, at other times he described it as a basic prop of Soviet power, a new form of worker-peasant alliance which is superior to war communism.

Lenin, as a marxist, naturally thought that freeing small-scale commodity production was a potential threat to the power of the proletariat. That is why he insisted on calling the consequences of NEP by their proper name – so that the party could consciously fight against them. But the great weakness of his position was that he could not create an explanatory link between the "irregularities" in the development of Soviet society and the "deformations" of the state power. Whenever he had to define what the danger was that threatened the dictatorship of the proletariat at the socio-economic level, he always mentioned the strengthening of the capitalist element; and whenever he defined what the danger was at the political level, he always talked about the bureaucratisation of the state. But he was unable to find a causal link between the two. He thought that bureaucratic excesses could be accounted for in three ways. First, the proletariat had been weakened as a class and was no longer capable of exercising power by itself; secondly, the Soviet state had no choice but to take over the tsarist bureaucracy together with its conditioning; and thirdly, since the Bolshevik officials did not have the education and experience to be able to rule, they could not effectively keep control over the apparatus which they had inherited from tsarism. None of these three reasons was connected with the economic restoration of capitalism. Rather, Lenin said that the Bolsheviks would have to learn the art of effective leadership from the capitalists, and would have to entrust capitalist entrepreneurs, where possible, with the effective organisation of economic processes. What is more, on one occasion he even went so far as to submit that it was the rise of capitalist industry that would give back to Russia a modern proletariat. When he thought about the threat involved in the strengthening of capitalism, he wanted to restrict the development of private enterprise; on the other hand, when he had to confront bureaucratisation, he sought to rely outright on private enterprise.

This paradoxical result clearly indicates that Lenin saw the increasing independence of the bureaucratic state machine as a problem of organisation and management, and not as a sociological problem. He could see clearly that it was not the proletariat which exercised power, but he did not ask himself the question, if the proletariat is not in power, which class is? In spite of everything, he was absolutely sure that even if it was not the working class that governed, the government represented the working class. Supreme power was held by the Bolshevik party's "old guard", the professional revolutionary élite which was incorruptible and had committed themselves once and for all to the cause of the proletariat. If they could stay in power until the world revolution, the dictatorship of the Russian proletariat would be saved.

For Lenin, the problem appeared to be that the will of the Bolshevik leaders came up against the organisational inertia of the apparatus, and that the decrees got lost in the bureaucratic labyrinth. Never for a moment did he think that the apparatus might tame the political leadership. This way of approaching the problem had dangerous consequences in practice: the greater the resistance of the bureaucratic apparatus to decrees from above, the greater the need of the "old guard" (according to Lenin) to maintain the appearance of unity. Only a foolproof unity could provide the "old guard" with the indisputable authority required for it to impose its will in spite of all the difficulties. Disclosure of the different policies which existed within the supreme leadership therefore had to be prevented at all costs.

According to the folklore of party history, just before his fatal stroke, Lenin was preparing a general offensive against Stalin, who was threatening democracy within the leadership; only his illness, which came "at the worst moment", prevented him from winning this battle. In reality, Lenin did not succeed in working out a position which would have enabled him to fight consistently — not against Stalin in person, but against the political phenomenon he represented. Whatever his personal sympathies were, there is no doubt that the weapons which Lenin had placed in Stalin's hands were as strong as — if not stronger than — those which he had placed in Trotsky's. But the myth of the "old guard" still enabled him personally, for the time being, to maintain the delicate balance between "the survival policy" and "the proletarian policy", between practical realism and theoretical orthodoxy.

Trotsky, Bukharin and Stalin

Already the power struggles which followed Lenin's illness and death upset this balance. The supreme leadership split in two, and the minority, which was in the process of being isolated, was forced to seriously consider the possibility that the sociological mechanisms of the apparatus might force purely proletarian principles to submit to its dominance, even within the "old guard". Trotsky could already see symptoms of the bureaucratisation of the party in the monolithic power of the "old guard" in 1923. The change turned out in fact to be even more dramatic: Trotsky was forced to realise that the changes in the Bolshevik party had not only a direct influence on the fate of the Russian revolution but also an indirect influence on the international revolutionary movement. Towards the middle of the 1920s the Comintern parties began one after the other to meet bitter failures. Trotsky could see clearly that these failures were systematic, and that they were related to the general Comintern policy which was directed from Russia. The approaching world revolution thus began to appear to Trotsky no longer as a simple external precondition for the victory of socialism in Russia: a change in Russian development itself was necessary if the world revolution was to turn objective possibility into practical reality.

From this point onwards, formulas such as "in spite of all the deformations", "in the last analysis", etc., were no use. However, this at least meant that they could no longer stand in the way of the search for causes behind the symptoms. All at once "bureaucracy" no longer meant simply "bureaucratism" but a vast apparatus organised on unified lines which was independent of social classes and subordinated the whole of society to it. From this point onwards it became possible to put together an explanatory theory concerning the relations between the socio-economic structure and the power structure. Trotsky borrowed the elements for this theory from Marx's analysis of the bonapartist state. At the beginning he took from Marx only the very general structure of the analysis, using it to account for the growing independence of the state apparatus by its role as intermediary between the various classes, i.e. between the classes of town and countryside. But he began to apply the analogy more and more closely. Like Marx, Trotsky set out from the same two hypotheses. First of all, the classes which had been capable of organising themselves politically were atomised; secondly, the power apparatus exploited this situation by presenting itself as the representative of the interests of a class which was not itself capable of political action and which stood in need of political tutelage from an autocratic state. In the period of "NEP excesses" Trotsky already had the impression that the Soviet bureaucracy was increasingly becoming a political rallying-point for the interests of the capitalist peasant economy, while the economically and numerically weaker proletariat was unable to impose its will.

Trotsky's practical programme followed directly from this explanation: the balance of forces between industry and agriculture had to change, so that the urban proletariat could once more subordinate the state apparatus to itself through the party and the councils. He therefore proposed that even if the free market in agricultural products could not be eliminated, at least the excess which was accruing to the peasant producers should be siphoned off and used to speed up industrial accumulation.

The weakest point in Trotsky's programme was without doubt his inability to point to the politically organised social force which would have been able and willing to carry it out. At first Trotsky sought chiefly to address himself to communist workers. But the attempt was destined to fail. His own analysis of the post-revolutionary situation showed that the workers' organisations at the base were too weak to resist manipulation by the apparatus. Obviously he could not think of relying on the peasantry. All he had left was to hope that his views would find an echo in that part of the apparatus where Bolshevik traditions were still alive. After he had been defeated in the base organisations, he was once again forced to try to address himself to the highest organs of the apparatus, while the very aim of his programme was to break its monolithic power.

But behind this practical inconsistency, which was generated by despair, lay a deeper theoretical inconsistency. The only reason why Trotsky could hope to strengthen the proletarian nature of power through accelerated industrialisation was because he saw the working class as merely a category of economic statistics and not as a political force which had acquired its consciousness through its own practice. For him it went without saying that an adequate class consciousness and an adequate level of organisation would emerge as soon as the economic weight of the working class grew. It did not occur to him that the historical process, the socio- and politico-economic institutions in which this new working class was being formed and its practical experiences, would be equally essential factors. It did not occur to him, because he too had no doubt that the existing system of institutions was, in terms of its original function, the embodiment of the dictatorship of the proletariat. He thought that the Soviet working class would no longer have to wear itself out in long struggles, errors and failures in order to reach an adequate level of organisation and class consciousness: both were given in the institutions and ideology of Soviet power. This is the deeper reason why Trotsky thought it possible to address himself to the apparatus with a programme which sought to restrict the power of this apparatus. He saw the bureaucracy not only as a privileged group acting in accordance with their particular interests, but also as the agent of an adequate class consciousness and of its corresponding organisation. This was why after Trotsky's political defeat he was stranded theoretically too – not because the apparatus rejected his programme, but because they put it into effect.

While Bukharin was telling the peasants "enrich yourselves!" the analogy with the bonapartist state could have seemed plausible. But several years later the régime made a sharp turn, crushed the peasantry brutally and launched a huge industrialisation programme. It was small consolation for Trotsky that in spite of the demented form which collectivism and industrialisation took it was nevertheless his own programme that was being put into effect. Neither the elimination of peasant smallholdings nor the creation of a large-scale industrial working class shook the power of the apparatus. On the contrary, the result was that the hegemony of the apparatus was extended to sectors of society which previously it had only been able to isolate and neutralise, without being able to control them directly. According to Marx, the bonapartist state relied on a social class which, because of its being atomised, was incapable of autonomous political action. After the turn, it became clear that the Soviet state did not need any such base. It was the state itself which was atomising the social classes, including those which – like the proletariat – were not atomised at the level of the social division of labour.

From the beginning of the 1930s onwards, Trotsky was no longer able to propose any autonomous programme of development alternative to the actual development of Soviet society and its economy. Nor was he able any longer to explain theoretically why the power of the ruling apparatus became general. He could only hover between two equally misleading predictions: sometimes he expected Soviet development to lead to the total restoration of capitalism, and sometimes he hoped that the economic basis of socialism would be realised in spite of everything.

As Bolshevik marxism was failing politically and being defeated theoretically, the apparatus's own ideology of "Soviet marxism" was gaining in consistency and importance. Before the appearance of the trotskyist opposition, the political debates had consisted of confrontations between the various doctrinal positions of the old Bolsheviks. The role of the apparatus in these debates was restricted to putting into effect the organisational consequences of what had been officially decided upon. The anti-Trotsky campaign was the first occasion on which the faceless mass membership of the apparatus emerged from their corners and played a leading role. For the first time, the tone and the outcome of the debate were determined by the propaganda machine and the organisational manoeuvring of the apparatus. The old Bolshevik leaders who rose against Trotsky were no more than participants in this huge general propaganda campaign. They were doing exactly the same thing as the hacks of the party press (though perhaps at a "higher" level): they chose from among Lenin's often contradictory statements those which could be used against Trotsky's proposals, and presented the affair as though two coherent and incompatible systems were locked in struggle, "leninism" and "trotskyism". They did not hesitate to falsify history in order to demonstrate that the struggle between the two "lines" had been going on permanently ever since the second congress of the Russian Social-Democratic Party. They calmly accused Trotsky of putting forward ideas which he had never held, and of having committed actions which he had never even contemplated.

But the old Bolsheviks were still careful to ensure that the conceptions they were declaring to be an organic part of "leninism" did not contradict Lenin's better-known texts. It was only Stalin who even at this point had no scruples about attributing ideas to Lenin that were incompatible with any positions Lenin had openly held. Trotsky stated that the more the world revolution was delayed the more tragic would be the deformations in the structure of Soviet power; it was then that Stalin dared to launch the slogan "Socialism in one country", claiming Lenin's authority. Zinoviev and Kamenev – who at that point were still Stalin's influential allies – denounced this fantastic heresy with saintly horror. This incident gave advance notice that it was Stalin who would be called upon to liquidate the theoretical traditions of marxist Bolshevism once and for all. But at this point Stalin did not play a big part in the ideological debates: it was Bukharin who took on the job of systematising and justifying the programme of the régime against Trotsky's.

Bukharin's conception clearly shows that the interests of the apparatus were having a definitive influence not only on the form of the debate but also on the content of official ideology. During the mid-1920s, when NEP achieved passing successes, it was not yet possible to win the apparatus over to a policy which would have suppressed Trotsky's attempts at democratisation at the same time as taking over his economic programme. The bureaucracy saw in the acceleration of industrial accumulation not only an imaginary risk that the proletariat would again become an autonomous political force, but also the real danger: the breakdown of the peasants' loyalty, which had been won at such a price, and the loss of its desire to produce. The apparatus had a tremendous fear of the peasant as a politically and economically unknown factor who could not be directly controlled. It thought it could coexist peacefully with the peasant by leaving the market to establish an equilibrium between industry and agriculture, and rejected as adventurism any attempt to interfere with the market equilibrium. The apparatus needed an ideology which would state that the social truce created by NEP could be indefinitely maintained: and such was precisely the theory Bukharin supplied it with.

Bukharin's thesis was that if the market equilibrium were overturned in the interests of accumulation, the peasantry would turn against the régime. Such measures were not necessary, in any case. The market should be left alone to establish freely the relation between agricultural and industrial income, and the kulak would end up being peacefully integrated into socialism. The kulak was an entrepreneur who sought to maximise his profits. The state therefore had simply to make it more profitable for him to take part in consumer, trading and credit co-operatives, so that whatever his political convictions he would join a co-operative system and tamely submit himself to the collective economy.

The apparatus was afraid of the peasants, and Bukharin told it that it could coexist with them by letting them enrich themselves. The apparatus wanted to delay confrontation as far as possible, and Bukharin told it that it could avoid confrontation. He discarded the theoretical traditions of marxism without any explanation whenever they did not correspond to what the apparatus wanted to hear. And yet Bukharin did not break completely with the traditions of Bolshevik marxism. The apparatus whose ideology he supplied had not yet subjected the society completely, and was still looking for a way to conform to the predictable behaviour of a class which was independent of it. It is true that Bukharin's predictions were based on the wishes of the apparatus and not on an analysis of class relations, but they were still couched in socio-economic terms, in a class language. The decisive turning-point only came when the apparatus decided to break the peasants' social and economic autonomy by force.

When new grain-requisitioning crises shook the régime in 1927 and 1928, it became clear that it was not enough to let the peasants enrich themselves, because this still did not guarantee that the towns would be supplied. From this point on, the apparatus began to fear what might happen if the peasants were left to do what they liked as much as what might happen if it tried to apply economic and political constraints to them. The idyllic picture of a market equilibrium no longer soothed their minds. Stalin's moment had come.

Bukharin had said that the more powerful the socialist forces became, the more probable it was that the kulak would be peacefully integrated into socialism. Stalin said that the kulak's resistance was proportional to the consolidation of socialism. If there were not enough wheat, he said, it was because the rich peasants wanted to starve the towns. The short-term result had to be forced requisitioning; in the long term, the state would create its own agricultural base. At least some of the peasant smallholdings must therefore be regrouped into collective organisations. But agricultural organisations of this type could only fully exploit the economies of scale by mechanising production. There was therefore a need for tractors and combine harvesters, and for this heavy industry was needed. Two things were therefore necessary: to collectivise agriculture and to speed up industrial accumulation.

It is hardly surprising that trotskyists were jubilant, and joined Stalin's camp one after another. The economic and political conclusions were their own, and Stalin's premises did not interest them. There was none the less something frightening about these premises, something which this time made the theoretical break with Bolshevik party tradition truly definitive. Stalin did not use the argument that under contemporary demographic conditions and at the given level of industrial and agricultural technology the peasant market and peasant smallholdings were incapable of feeding the country regularly. Instead, he invented the story that the kulaks were organising themselves against Soviet power, that they were hoarding their grain. The so-called growing resistance of the kulaks appeared to Stalin to be a conspiracy, a secret plot by invisible forces. The behaviour of this social group was not determined by the manifest interest which was rooted in its own economic and social situation, but by provocateurs hidden somewhere in the shadows. It did not act as a class, but as a "class enemy".

As soon as clandestine organisations, enemy propaganda and sabotage were put forward as explanations of social behaviour, the boundaries between the classes lost their theoretical importance. The kulak was not the only enemy: the local official who did not find as much grain in his village as the central organs calculated he should was also an enemy, or at least an accomplice. There were other enemy accomplices: the engineer whose tractor factory could not be run at the excessive tempo required from above, the economist who said that one could not invest a greater part of the gross national product than that which remained after allowing for consumption and reproduction, the worker who was unable to fulfil raised norms. It mattered little whether it was complicity, leniency or lack of vigilance: anyone who did not measure up to official expectations was part of the great plot. The socio-economic point of view was replaced by a police point of view, and the measures taken against classes became police measures rather than economic and political ones. In the end there was no longer any need to link even verbally with any class, they simply became "the class enemy", "Menshevik provocateurs" or "trotskyist-bukharinist agents".

Stalinism was the ideology of the turn, in the course of which the apparatus extended its rule by force over all those sectors of society which it did not yet directly control. The apparatus no longer had any interest in predicting the behaviour of independent classes, because all classes were subject to its authority. What was important was that the shocks which accompanied the changes should not disintegrate the power system. There had to be systematic mass terror, so that no one should even dream of resisting any more. Marxist ideology, having functioned more or less well up to that time as a class theory with claims to be predictive, became an instrument of terror above all classes.

The Bolshevik canonisation of marxism

As the class theory withered away along with its predictive pretensions, Soviet marxism canonised the grotesque cosmology and general methodology which have until the present day determined the system of presenting and inculcating marxism in Eastern Europe. As the marxist theory of society was drained of its content, so what was called "dialectical materialism" gained ground in the ideology which had to justify the decisions of the régime. The most important Bolshevik theoreticians of the 1920s – Lenin, Trotsky and Bukharin – also had well-defined positions on general philosophical questions. Lenin attributed a special importance to general issues of philosophy in safeguarding the specifically marxist nature of the Bolshevik party. But none of them sought to deduce the party's practical strategy from a dialectical methodology or cosmology. Their practical orientation was based on the analysis of Russian society and the realities of international capitalism, with the help of marxist economics and the marxist theory of classes. It was only after Marx's theory of classes had been emptied of its content and "dialectical materialism" had been canonised that the general philosophy of nature and the methodology attributed to marxism assumed a direct political importance.

The content of this doctrine is well-known to anyone who has graduated in an East European country or who has attended party seminars there; and it is not unknown in the West, although it has never taken precedence over social theory in the educational and theoretical work of the West European parties. The absurdity of the doctrine is evident to any marxist able to think for himself, although there have always been people – chiefly marxist neophytes from Western intellectual milieux – for whom it is precisely the grotesque character of "dialectical materialism" that exercises a kind of psychological attraction: the more meaningless and primitive the ideas they hold, the more certain they are that they have succeeded in breaking with bourgeois science and culture. But this is simply a farcical repetition of what was once a tragedy.

During the stalinist era, the cosmology of "dialectical materialism" was the background music which accompanied systematic mass terror. The struggle between contradictions which always dominate their unity raised the theory of sharpening class struggle to the level of a cosmic law. The dialectic of quantity and quality, which always takes place in "leaps", dressed up as cosmic necessity the political turns required by problems of balancing the economy and by the unscrupulous pragmatism of foreign policy. The "dialectical materialist" methodology meant nothing more than to raise ambiguity to the level of a systematic principle; it was a methodology that enabled symbolic links to be created between the régime's individual decisions and the final aims of socialism. Under the given "concrete conditions", any measure which was apparently contrary to the objectives of socialism might correspond "in the last analysis" to those very same objectives. If anyone did not carry out these measures, whatever his motives, he was "objectively" against socialism. And the very fact that "dialectical materialism" subordinated historical materialism as one particular case of the application of its own universally valid laws meant that social processes appeared as natural necessities. The examination of alternatives, the choice between various possibilities of action and the responsibility for what follows, all this was eliminated from social praxis. Praxis was reduced to the status of adapting to necessity, although this does not exclude the possibility (and anyone who has a grain of "dialectics" in them can see this) that problems of adaptation may occur, problems which have to be eliminated as radically as possible in the name of conscious necessity.

This cosmological and methodological edifice built by the marxism of the apparatus fulfilled a very important ideological function in stalinist policy. However, it would be a serious mistake to deduce from this that the entire content of "dialectical materialism" was determined by this function. The thesis of sharpening class struggle could stand on its own feet; it was not absolutely necessary to turn it into a cosmology. The naturalistic interpretation of social praxis would in principle have been much easier to elaborate without taking any elements from Hegel, in a more modern and scientistic conception such as that which Bukharin attempted to advance. And in such a conception, one might also have included the necessity of sharp turns (though not Bukharin's textbook *Historical Materialism*, for his theory of equilibrium was too close to his political programme). In reality what happened was not that the primitive class theory which looks on society from the policeman's point of view was supplemented with a cosmology conforming to stalinist policy. "Dialectical materialism" had already been fully formed during the debates of the 1920s, as a kind of academic theory relatively independent of factional struggles, even if the debates themselves were not conducted in a fair academic manner. After the turn took place, "dialectical materialism" was adapted to the new political slogans and was used as an underlying theme, whereas previously the theory was only of interest to education and science.

The content of educational marxism was determined by two factors: first of all, by the conception of marxist philosophy which sprang from the theoretical traditions of Bolshevism (chiefly Lenin's writings on philosophy), and later, by the exceptionally important role of philosophy in the struggle through which the apparatus extended its power over scientific and cultural life.

The specific philosophical traditions of Bolshevism go back to the years following the 1905 revolution. During this period, when the unity of the weakened Bolshevik faction was threatened by political debates that were already quite violent, Lenin put extreme emphasis on abstract philosophical questions which bore no relation (or only a very indirect one) to the practical tasks of Russian social democracy. The strangeness of this attitude did not escape some of his contemporaries, but no one has so far succeeded in finding a satisfactory explanation. This would require a serious critical analysis of the contemporary sources, so let us restrict ourselves to certain cautious hypotheses.

On the whole, the Russian social democrats never thought of their separation into two factions as final until the polarisation which took place after the February revolution. It was only after February that Bolsheviks and Mensheviks mobilised the masses against their respective political organisations in order to conquer the political positions occupied by the opposing organisation. Previously the separation had never gone beyond the fact that active revolutionaries were loyal to this or that particular group of leaders, the question of membership of a particular faction of the organisation, or the adoption of debating positions on tactical and programmatic questions. In its work among the masses, each faction of the organisation was busy creating and maintaining its own base among the urban workers and intellectuals. Even after the upturn of 1912 the mass movements were spontaneous; they were not led by one of these organisations and therefore did not reflect the differences in the tactics and programme of the two factions. It is true that the two factions presented different sets of candidates with different slogans at elections, but it was the superior strength of the common enemy which determined the behaviour of those elected, not the difference between their programmes. In general even the social democratic members of the Duma were careful to prevent the internal divisions within their small group from extending to the public sphere.

In these conditions, the fact that the Bolshevik faction had worked out a more or less official position on abstract theoretical questions of no political consequence could have been useful from several points of view. First of all, there was the numerical weakness of the party's mass base. For a party controlling large masses of people (for example, an organisation as powerful as the German Social Democratic Party, the pride of the workers' movement at that time), it was even preferable, from a political point of view, to adopt a liberal attitude towards general philosophical questions. This enabled it to win over a section of those social groups which were alien to the dominant philosophical traditions of the early socialists. In the practice of such parties it was not philosophical orthodoxy that guaranteed political intransigence but the class adherence of the organised masses, as well as the relation of the workers' movement to antagonistic organistions representing opposed social interests. This sociological guarantee was missing in Bolshevism, which was isolated from the masses and organisationally weak. Under such conditions the most abstract philosophical questions were able to have a particular significance for the maintenance of the party's class commitment. There was in fact a fear that the attempts to "reorientate marxism on a modern philosophical basis" which had become fashionable after the failure of the 1905 revolution might lead to conclusions in social theory which would have dire consequences for the practical orientation of the party. Secondly, the development of an official philosophical position could play some part in the Bolshevik faction's fierce battle for an autonomous identity. One should always change the tactics and the programme according to changes in the situation, but one can always hang on to philosophical positions which do not have direct practical relevance.

But whether these hypotheses are correct or not, the fact remains that Lenin succeeded in imposing his own view that marxism contains a specific philosophy of nature, theory of perception and methodology, and that for the active militant acceptance or rejection of them was no private matter. And this had its consequences in the post-revolutionary Soviet system. If the demand for a particular philosophical doctrine became part and parcel of the Bolshevik ideological tradition, then the marxism of the apparatus — one of whose chief functions is its symbolic representation of fidelity to the traditions — could not turn down this demand. It is necessary to interpret the texts of Marx, Engels and Lenin on which this demand is based: the results thus obtained must be formulated in such a way that they can be used without ambiguity in education and propaganda. At the point when these tasks were being carried out, in the 1920s, big differences still kept appearing, although no one challenged the need for a specifically marxist system of the philosophy of nature. Two schools formed, the "dialecticians" and the "mechanicists" — but both fought for a monopoly of the official philosophy.

Tradition influenced the outcome of the struggle decisively. The publication of Lenin's *Philosophical Notebooks* and of some of Engels's manuscripts swung the balance in favour of the "dialecticians". But there was another factor which played a part in their victory. The apparatus could only extend its power gradually, even in cultural and scientific life. The most difficult part of the intelligentsia to control was that which was openly committed to Soviet rule on basic political questions and, because of this, felt entitled to elaborate autonomously and on its own terrain the science and culture appropriate to the new society. The apparatus could not impose a simple political discipline on the left intelligentsia; if it wanted to put an end to their autonomy, which might become politically dangerous, it had to intervene in specific cultural and scientific questions. It was official philosophy's job to justify such an intervention: marxism is a universal philosophy, from it follows a specific position on all scientific and cultural questions, and it goes without saying that doctrinal purity can only be preserved by the acting heir of marxist doctrine, the party itself.

The "dialecticians" held advantages from this point of view too. Their opponents, the "mechanicists", simply wanted the scientific *Weltanschauung* to become the *Weltanschauung* of the proletariat; for them, it was not marxist tradition but the latest findings of science that had to constitute the basis of a universalist marxist philosophy. The "dialecticians", on the other hand, set out from the proposition that the "dialectical method" drawn from Hegel by Marx, Engels and Lenin had universal authority, including in the natural sciences. The really important findings of modern science were due to the fact that their discoverers had followed (unconsciously, of course) this dialectical method. But because they only did so unconsciously, on philosophical questions they were usually still idealists – which was not just ideologically dangerous but could also hold back the progress of science itself. It therefore became necessary for scientists to consciously adopt and apply the "dialectical materialist" theory of knowledge.

However, this adaptation to the requirements of the apparatus's scientific and cultural policy shaped the "dialectical" position itself. At the beginning of the debate, while the "mechanicists" were trying to work out a concrete scientific *Weltanschauung*, the "dialecticians" were simply proposing a methodology and combating so-called idealist interpretations of scientific theory. Gradually, the two positions were reversed. The "mechanicists" went on the defensive and tried to demonstrate that the methodological principles of the "dialecticians" were trivial or that they led nowhere, while the methods disclosed in the course of scientific discovery were fruitful. But their opponents, who were gradually gaining the upper hand, transformed methodological principles into ontological ones. The apparatus seized on this stage in the evolution of the debate, because it needed precisely the kind of instrument that would enable it to declare any theory it liked as incompatible with marxism. And the fact that the theses of "dialectical materialism" were trivial or nonsensical was a definite advantage: they were only needed when political necessity demanded it, and they did not have any logically meaningful implications.

After the turn, there was simply an eventual canonisation of the system of official marxist philosophy, which was adapted to stalinist policy. But the adaptation was not perfect. First, the specific philosophical theses which stalinist philosophy employed were chosen accidentally according to the historical situation which prevailed at the time of the choice. And secondly, the tradition contained certain very annoying elements: for example its positive judgement on Hegel, the consequences of which had to be fought over and over again. But the strongest and most persistent tension came from the fact that although this system of official philosophy could be used to justify the most arbitrary measures in politics, culture and science perfectly well, its very objectivism in fact contradicted the excessive voluntarism of stalinist policy. This tension sometimes allowed people to appeal to "objective truth" in order to defend certain scientific and cultural values against the apparatus. What is more, Stalin himself towards the end of his life played with the contradiction between objectivism and voluntarism; he loved to appear as if it were not he who was responsible for "voluntarist" excesses.

The rebirth of marxism

Once stalinist ideology had been codified, the fate of a marxism founded on the same basis as the system appeared to be sealed for good in Eastern Europe. One might have expected that the ruling apparatus, whose weight had pulverised the theory of classes that formed the backbone of the marxist tradition, would nip in the bud any attempt to return to the problems specific to marxism and to restore its specific practical role. But that is not exactly what happened. Towards the middle of the 1950s the ideological debates flared up again, and in the course of these debates the internal dimensions of marxism began to reassert themselves. The accent gradually shifted towards the social sciences, or at least towards social philosophy (there were even voices explicitly raised against the idea of a philosophy of nature specific to marxism); there was a demand for marxism to break radically with everything that had been used to justify the terror, and for a return to the original sources – Marx, Lenin, or even the Lukács of the 1920s.

What made this new turn possible was the dislocation of the régime after Stalin's death, when the political unity of the ruling class around the apparatus was disintegrating, a unity which for a long time had been maintained only by systematic terror. A large group of the ruling class wanted to form a new administrative system. This new system would not do away with the apparatus's monopoly of power, but it would not be based on systematic mass terror and would give greater autonomy to the lower strata of the ruling class. That part of the political élite whose power was directly connected with the application of terror naturally resisted these attempts at reform with all its might. The faction which favoured the reforms (and which wanted power) tried to prevent the restoration of the former élite by denouncing the crimes of stalinism publicly, and it was prepared to use any means whatever to do so: this included the authorisation of public debates. It allowed accounts of the concentration camps to be published, it approved historical analyses of the strategic mistakes committed at the beginning of the second world war, it permitted economic criticisms of forced accumulation, and it even helped to publicise attacks on "dialectical materialism". At moments of exacerbation in the political struggle it became possible to a certain extent to cultivate a marxism that no longer served ritual aims only but allowed tangible and meaningful conclusions.

But the fact that it was not in the interest of any groups in the ruling class to reveal the class base and power structure of the stalinist era determined the precise route taken by this new marxism which had reacquired a social content. At no point was there any support for a radical criticism which tried to understand the specifics of stalinist policy by the way of relations between the apparatus and the basic social classes. No one even put forward the idea that the historical direction of stalinist policy was the extension of the power of the apparatus to all classes and all spheres of social life. But if it was not put forward, this was not simply because public discussion of such ideas would have gone beyond the bounds of the political tolerance of the new ruling stratum in its struggle to consolidate its own power. Marxists who were fighting to end the system of terror themselves felt that to reveal the class antagonisms of Soviet-type societies would only help the conservative and restorationist forces. Moreover, stalinist ideology had justified the system of terror precisely by dramatising class antagonisms. It was for this reason that the critics of the system of terror were insistent on the social homogeneity of Soviet-type societies. Their critique was based on the hypothesis that the social antagonisms which still existed were no threat to the established institutional system, and that it was therefore unnecessary to suppress them by force; the apparatus should set society the kind of aims in which the interests of the different social strata would converge, and should fulfil these aims by methods which would make the convergence of their interests real and evident to these social strata.

The marxism of the thaw thus sidestepped the problem of basic class antagonism, and that is why it denied itself *ab ovo* the opportunity of continuing the critical analysis at least from the level where the Bolshevik opposition of the 1920s had been forced to stop. First, the social objectives with which it was concerned were more general than any specific class aspirations. It elaborated that aspect of social ideals which enabled socialism to be interpreted as the desired aim of everyone, of humanity as a whole, and contrasted these ideals with the "deformations" of the stalinist era. Secondly, the realisation of these objectives appeared to the marxists of the thaw to be a technical and organisational problem. In the countries of Eastern Europe, these objectives were not contradicted by the interests of any social group, and the great majority of the ruling group was deeply committed to them. The people who had profited directly from stalinist policies, for whom the reforms were a disadvantage or an outright threat that the issue of responsibility would be raised, were in a minority compared with ordinary party members who had carried out the directives of the stalinist government in good faith and with the illusion that they were acting in the interests of socialism. The task was therefore simply to find which instruments would genuinely be capable of carrying out socialist objectives.

In this interpretation stalinist policies appeared to be a gigantic historical misunderstanding. Its foundations were chiefly ideological: the deformation and misapplication of marxist principles. The social causes usually invoked – backwardness, isolation, and their consequences – were simply the sparks which set off this misunderstanding. And now that they had essentially ceased to apply, the fate of the reforms would no longer depend on anything but the correction of mistakes, the ideological self-criticism of the system: it was only this *a posteriori* criticism that introduced a fully instrumentalist interpretation of the philosophical system crowning stalinist ideology. If the political "deformations" stemmed from certain ideological errors, they had to be errors which had materialised in theories which are very effective and very dangerous. And during the period of reforms, marxists pounced on every single piece of stalinist ideological bric-à-brac that could possibly be credited with being so effective.

They discussed in deadly earnest even the most grotesque theses of the "dialectical materialist" cosmology. This time they were concerned with finding examples which show that the contradictions have more peaceful "non-antagonistic" variants, and that not every gradual change necessarily culminates in a "leap". They took up again, one by one, all the "dialectical materialist" theses that had been used to justify repression against various scientific schools and tendencies. And they discovered that all they had to do was interpret them correctly for all the modern sciences to become easily reconcilable with "dialectical materialism". With great solemnity they came up with trivial generalities – for example, the idea that the social conditioning of human action does not exclude the existence of alternatives, and that it is possible to choose between these alternatives. They employed an immense interpretative apparatus to demonstrate that the sociological and political realism of the marxist "classics" did not imply a cynical relativism in ethical questions.

Of course, even the most naïve representatives of the marxism of the thaw knew that the social consequences of what were known as theoretical errors could not be got rid of simply by means of an ideological purge, by changes in the political objectives and the removal of the diehard stalinists. The mistaken policies had also deformed society's institutional system. But here too, it was simply a question of "deformations." The system of economic and political institutions is adequate to the homogeneity of society, so that it is not necessary to radically transform it. It would suffice to change the bureaucratic methods of leadership, and it is enough to bring back democratic decision-making and supervisory mechanisms that in the formal sense are already built into the structural principles of the existing institutions and organisations. However sharp the expression of these criticisms – and they often required a great deal of personal courage – the marxists of the thaw did not succeed in recognising that these mechanisms, highly democratic in their form, did not offer even the formal possibility of a political crystallisation of the real antagonisms of society.

Underground marxism versus official marxism

The sociological and political naïvety of the marxism of destalinisation was nourished by the quick-blooming hopes of a society reborn after systematic terror was stopped. It would be unhistorical to fail to see the real heroism in it. It was this that eventually drove some marxists to go beyond the critique of stalinist ideology, on the grounds that the internal structure of this critique is still determined by the object criticised, that is to stay by stalinist ideology itself. These marxists try to analyse the traditions systematically, to rethink all the principles that have previously been counterposed to stalinism.

For them, the study of Marx's texts is no longer simply a way of finding authorised counter-arguments to the inhuman consequences of the cosmology of "dialectical materialism". The reaffirmation of freedom of action and of the responsibility for human action is no longer simply a defence against the determinism which makes everything seem inevitable and therefore justifiable. The new philosophy which has sprung from the marxism of the thaw is no longer content with the opportunity to state certain truths (trivial in themselves) about the human condition. These truths, drawn from the writings of the young Marx, make up a positive system which is anthropological and philosophico-historical: by his very nature, man is a free social being. The specificities of his biological nature and of his natural environment determine the cultural environment which guarantees his survival, but only as negative, limiting conditions. Within these limits, men create their culture by their own interrelated actions and by building on each other's results. But from the philosophico-historical standpoint, this anthropological fact appears as a possibility that only results from a long process of evolution. So far throughout the history of humanity, the evolution of society has not been determined by the freely chosen and consciously co-ordinated objectives of man. The results of previous evolution have dominated society as a second nature. The opportunity for human beings to exercise conscious and collective control over the evolution of their social life has only appeared now, in the historical present. The appearance of this possibility, at least in a historically favourable part of the globe, is the result of objective tendencies of evolution. But the exploitation of this opportunity is a practical question, and is not guaranteed by any set of objective circumstances in themselves.

We have given only the bare outlines of this anthropological and philosophico-historical conception, since we do not have the opportunity to give an account of all its individual variations or nuances. It therefore appears more abstract than it is in fact. But this should not take us away from the essential question. It is precisely the abstract nature of this philosophy of praxis, which has sprung from the marxism of the thaw, that enables it to make a more radical critique of Soviet-type societies. In the most general sense, it rejects the substitutionism in all the variations of official marxism, traces of which are also to be found in the marxism of the thaw: the apparatus and the party run society in the name and in the interests of the working class (or, according to the marxists of the thaw, in the interests of "the people" or "human beings"), and the socialist character of society depends on the correctness of this leadership. But in the view of the philosophy of praxis, a society can only be socialist if it is run by "human beings" themselves. It is no accident that no one talks about anything but "human beings" any more. The philosophy of praxis in Eastern Europe, borrowing heavily from the young Marx and from Western marxist philosophy of the 1920s, is on this point a continuation of the marxism of the thaw: the subject of praxis is undefined from a class point of view.

The general humanist enthusiasm of the marxism of the thaw sprang from a reaction to stalinist ideology and from the as yet undifferentiated hopes of a society just freed from systematic terror. But by the time the philosophy of praxis was developing out of the marxism of the thaw these motives were already stripped of their effectiveness. In the consolidating post-stalinist system, the object of this type of criticism — ideology in the service of terror — was being forgotten. The thesis of sharpening class struggle has officially been rejected, verbal adherence to the dictatorship of the proletariat is being abandoned, the Soviet state is proclaimed to be the "state of all the people", and finally the official ideology has been rid of those last indirect references which, if only by contrast, alluded to the vocabulary of terror. The only positive function left for the official ideology is the symbolic representation of continuity in the institutions of power. Beyond this, marxism no longer has more than a negative role: it hides the class structure of society and prevents any public and critical class analysis of the nature of power, social inequalities and the lack of individual and collective freedoms. And in the post-stalinist régime, the hopes of "human beings" themselves are also differentiated: each social stratum has found the route which will enable it to make use of the opportunities provided by the new system, in accordance with its own situation. And the particular aspirations of these groups cannot be harmonised with marxist humanism at the philosophical level, and sometimes contradict it outright.

Those strata of the ruling class which have directed the

post-stalinist transformation no longer even worry about referring to marxist traditions when they justify the elimination of terror. The criticism belongs to the past at the point where they are already working for the realisation of their own aims, for which they need the ideology of market socialism. This ideology inevitably enters into conflict with any kind of marxism that seeks to draw tangible conclusions for the interpretation of Soviet-type societies from an examination of the "classic" texts.

For the intellectuals, "marxism" is the name given to the limits which are imposed on their free creative work. It is possible to do something within the limits, and one can even gradually extend them: but one cannot go beyond them. Experience demonstrates that every initiative in this direction has provoked a tightening of the rope. The abstract radicalism of philosophers who dare to explore the forbidden areas of marxism leads only to risk and danger for the vast majority of intellectuals.

And finally, the most important thing is that the divergences between the philosophy of praxis and official marxism in no way relate to the working class. During the struggle for the elimination of terror, the ideological differences could be directly translated into alternatives of everyday life for the working class: the moralising humanism of the marxists of the thaw meant the end of permanent mobilisation and a rise in the level of consumption, while the pseudo-hegelian and pseudo-scientific determinism of the stalinists meant a return to the use of extra-economic force and absolute pauperisation. But under the post-stalinist system, which has already been stabilised, the alternatives are no longer so simple and clearcut, and one can no longer connect the empirical interests of the working class with the various positions adopted in the sphere of philosophical abstraction. But even if the working class could extract some kind of message from the philosophy of praxis, this message would never reach it. All communication between the marxist intelligentsia and the working class has once again been made impossible, because the gates of the information channels and organisation have been closed again.

The philosophy of praxis sought to be the philosophy of

man, that is to say of all men: but at the point when it assumed a form, it found no echo with anyone. The ruling class answers radical political conclusions with repression, even when they are abstract. And those who do not bow to this repression must either emigrate or go underground. But this time political defeat and theoretical failure will not end in general annihilation, as they did after the liquidation of the Bolshevik opposition in the 1920s. It is true that the social influence of marxism has become infinitely weaker. But at least marxist thought survives underground. And what is more important, this new situation in which the nonconformist marxists find themselves enables them to draw positive lessons from the defeat they have suffered. Illusions about the class structure and institutions of Soviet-type societies are dissolving, and it seems less and less likely that the marxism which disengages itself from the official ideology will see its practical duty in seeking to instruct or enlighten any group of the ruling class. The obstacles which used to prevent criticism in the terms of the theory of class from being concretely carried out are disappearing. The way is open for a search for the autonomous social base of marxism.

Of course, if East European marxism is to find its connection with the working class in practice, and if by its own theoretical means it is to help the process of practical learning in which the socialist movement – organised and possessing a class consciousness – spreads to an increasingly large part of the working class, it is not enough for marxist intellectuals simply to lose their illusions about the ruling class. There must also be such changes in the organisation of society and in the situation of the working class that the institutions of power are no longer strong enough to fragment the working class. Until these changes can be foreseen, the marxism which has definitively broken away from official marxism is threatened with disappearance, or with dissolution among the non-marxist underground ideologies which are better suited to the social isolation of the nonconformist intelligentsia. But at least it has succeeded in avoiding the trap of trying to live as a parasite on official marxist ideology.

Index

Accumulation, 11, 29, 36, 108
Agriculture, 13, 29, 122
Antique mode of production, 16
Asiatic mode of production, 16

Bukharin, N. I., 118, 120, 121, 125
Bureaucracy, 10, 12, 45, 46, 108, 114, 116, 118, 120

Capitalism, contemporary, 11, 15, 73-104 *passim*; Marx's view of, 16, 17
Capitalist property, 10, 15
China, 16
Comintern, 17, 74, 116
Consumer behaviour, 14, 35
Consumer goods, 23-4, 30, 31, 33, 35-6, 37, 54, 75, 92, 93-5, 96-7
Co-operatives, agricultural, 122
Czechoslovakia, 9, 32, 63
Decentralisation, 19, 25, 31, 33, 36, 63, 81, 86, 92, 101, 102
Decision-making, 20-22, 25, 30, 36, 77, 86, 101, 134
Dialectical materialism, 8, 68, 124-6, 129, 131, 133, 134
Division of labour, 16-17, 28, 73, 75, 86, 88, 91

Elite, political, 20-21, 26, 29, 30-32, 33-5, 43, 50, 51, 52-4, 86, 87, 93, 102, 131
Engels, Friedrich, 49, 128, 129
Enterprise directors, 22, 23, 25, 27, 34, 54, 81. *See also* Managers
Experts, 21, 22, 28

Fascism, 13, 83

Gdansk massacre, 9
German Democratic Republic, 36, 63
Germanic mode of production, 16

Hegel, G. W. F., 125, 129, 130
Hierarchy, 14, 21, 22, 23, 25, 27-8, 44, 45, 46, 52, 56, 57, 77, 80, 81-9 *passim*, 101, 103, 108
Historical materialism, 8, 15, 17
Historicism, 15, 16, 17
Hungary, 9, 30, 32, 63

India, 16
Industry and industrialisation, 9, 13, 29, 50, 74, 108, 117, 118, 120
Intellectuals and intelligentsia, 8, 10, 19, 39-72, 75, 90-91, 128-9, 137, 138

Kamenev, L. B., 120
Kautsky, Karl, 110
Kulaks, 121, 122, 123

Lenin, V. I., 108, 113-16, 119-20, 124, 126, 128, 129, 131
Leninism, 9, 130
Lukács, Georg, 131

Managers and management, 20, 21-3, 26-7, 30, 31, 33, 34 ff., 43, 54-5, 57, 63, 85, 86, 93, 98, 101, 102-3
Marginalisation, 55-7, 62, 64, 65
Market socialism, 18-38, 137
Marx, Karl, 15-16, 17, 116, 118, 128, 129, 131, 134, 135, 136

Military dictatorships, 83

NEP (New Economic Policy), 106, 113, 117, 120, 121

Peasantry, 107-8, 109, 117, 118, 120, 121-2
Philosophy, Bolshevik traditions of, 126, 127, 129
Plekhanov, G. V., 110
Poland, 30, 32, 36, 63
Praxis, philosophy of, 125, 135-6, 137-8

Research, scientific, 43, 45, 49, 51, 52, 56, 57-8, 60, 62, 89-90, 92
Ruling class, 21, 24, 26, 28, 29ff., 33-5, 37, 42, 47, 52, 53-4, 83-6, 88, 91, 93, 99, 100, 101-3, 105, 106-7, 131, 136, 138
Rumania, 36
Russia. *See* Soviet Union

Second International, 17, 110, 111
Soviet Union, 7, 9, 10, 13, 39-42, 50, 62, 63-4, 70, 72, 76, 91, 106-38
Stalin, J. V., 41, 102, 110, 115, 120, 122, 130, 131
Stalinism, 9, 13, 29, 31, 32, 35, 48-9, 50, 52, 53, 56, 60, 123, 131
State capitalism, theory of, 7, 11, 14
Sub-intelligentsia, 60-62, 64, 68

Technocracy, 11
Technology, 51, 74-5, 87, 91-2
Technostructure, 11, 14, 91
Transitional society, theory of, 9, 10, 12ff., 42
Trotsky, L. D., 10, 108, 115, 116-20
Trotskyism, 12, 68

Workers' councils, 66
Working class, 7, 8, 10, 14, 21, 28, 33, 34, 35, 37, 38, 42, 54, 65-6, 71, 83, 88, 91, 96, 100, 103, 105, 108, 111-112, 114, 118, 136, 137

Zinoviev, G. I., 120

LIBRARY OF DAVIDSON COLLEGE

...hecked out for **two weeks.** Books